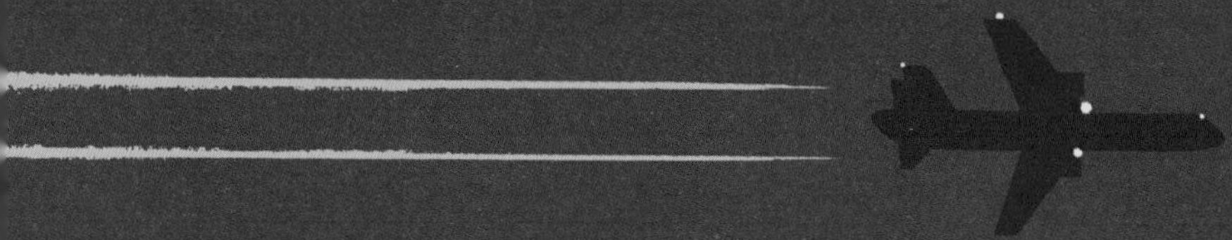

# Killing and Dying

Killi

and

Dyin

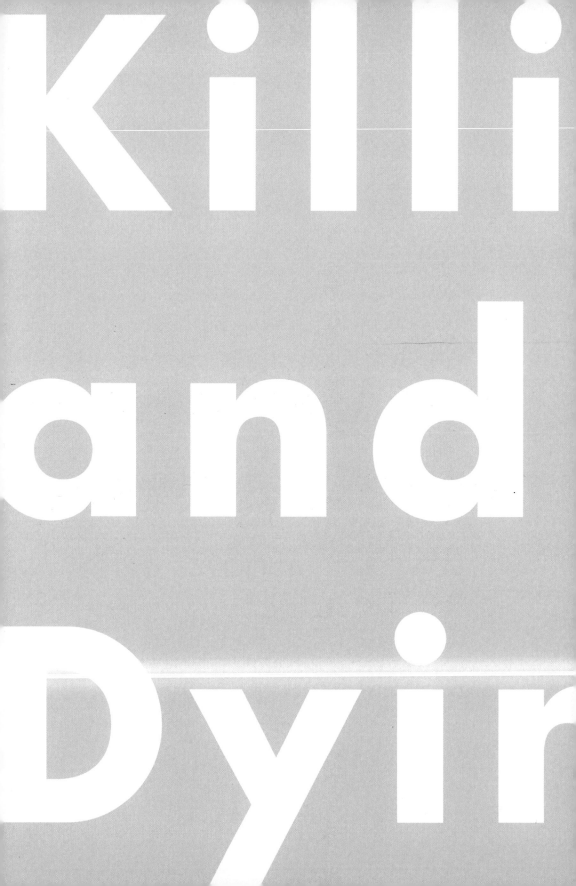

SIX STORIES BY ADRIAN TOMINE

*Drawn & Quarterly*

ALSO BY ADRIAN TOMINE

*Sleepwalk and Other Stories*

*32 Stories: The Complete Optic Nerve Mini-Comics*

*Summer Blonde*

*Scrapbook (Uncollected Work: 1990–2004)*

*Shortcomings*

*Scenes from an Impending Marriage*

*New York Drawings*

FOR CHRIS AND SATSUKI

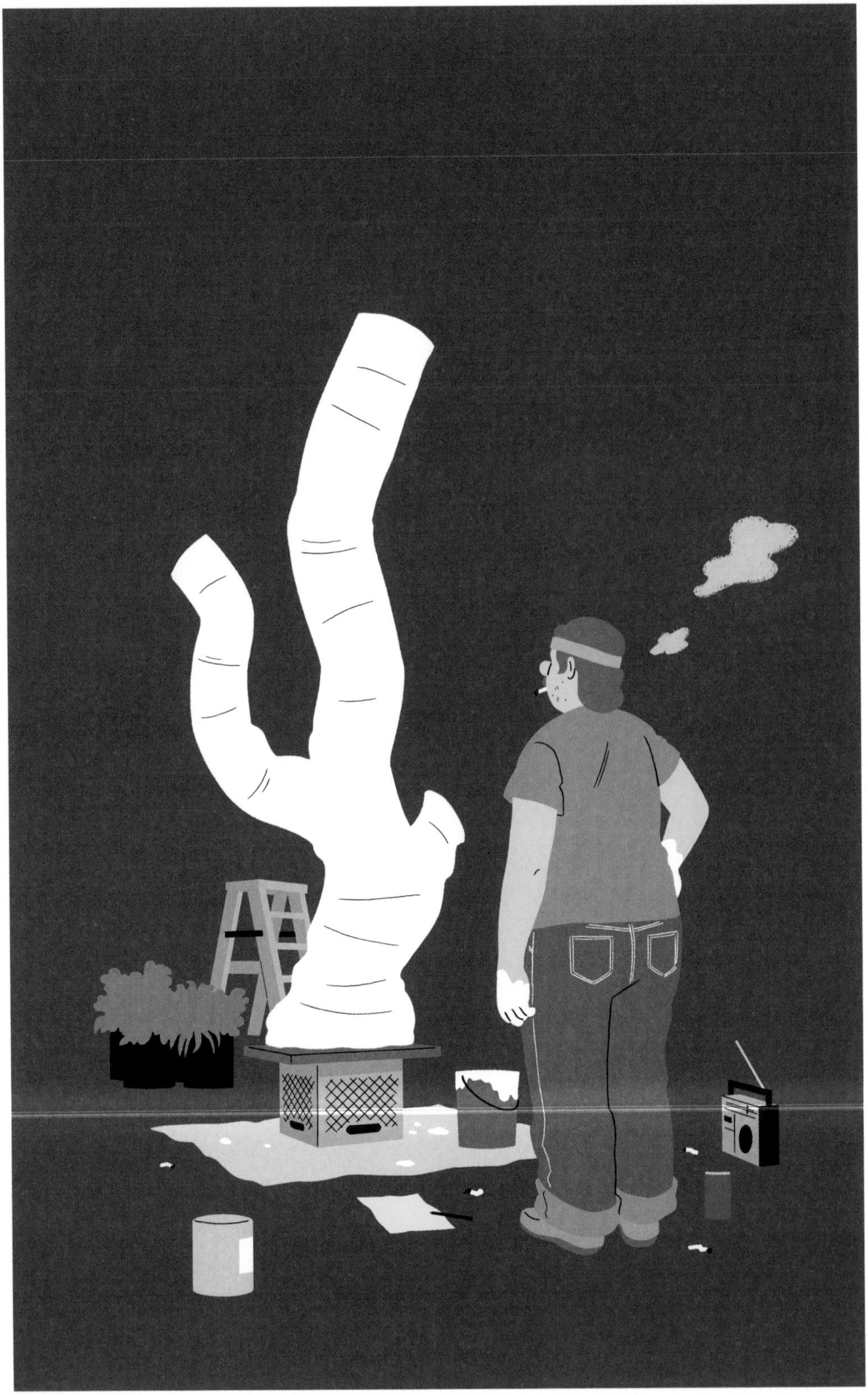

# CONTENTS

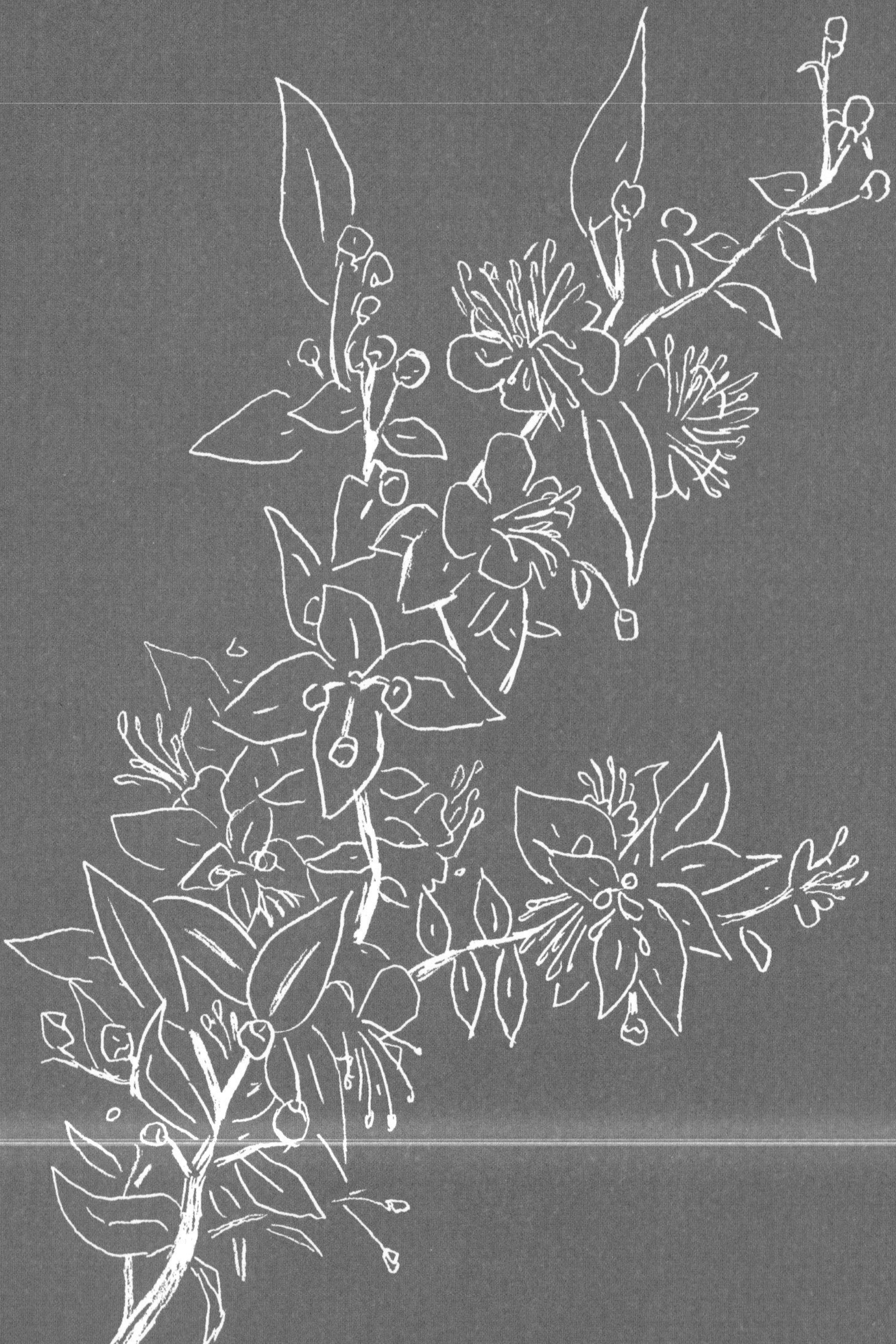

A BRIEF HISTORY of
the ART FORM KNOWN as
"HORTISCULPTURE"

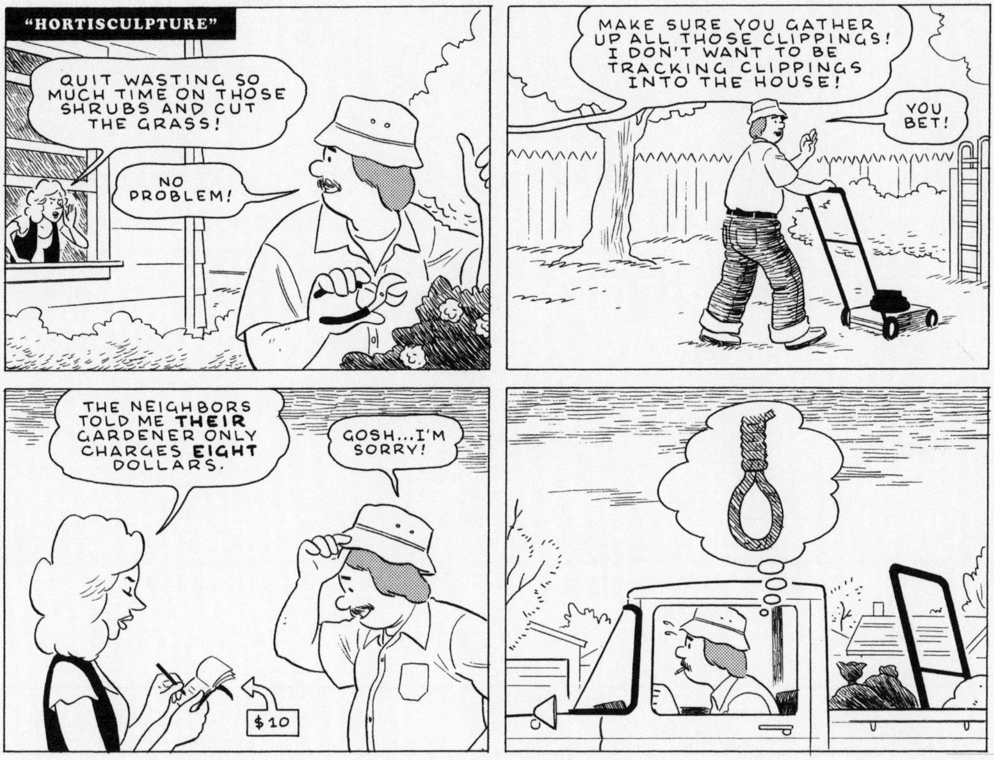
"HORTISCULPTURE"
QUIT WASTING SO MUCH TIME ON THOSE SHRUBS AND CUT THE GRASS!
NO PROBLEM!
MAKE SURE YOU GATHER UP ALL THOSE CLIPPINGS! I DON'T WANT TO BE TRACKING CLIPPINGS INTO THE HOUSE!
YOU BET!
THE NEIGHBORS TOLD ME THEIR GARDENER ONLY CHARGES EIGHT DOLLARS.
GOSH...I'M SORRY!
$10

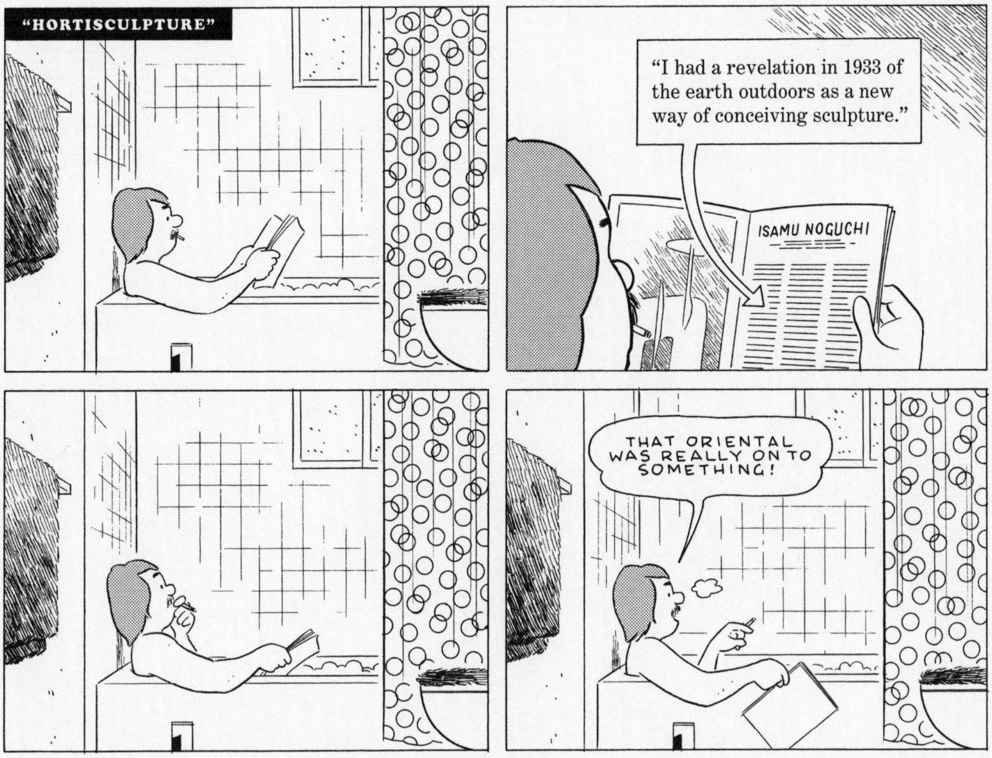
"HORTISCULPTURE"
"I had a revelation in 1933 of the earth outdoors as a new way of conceiving sculpture."
ISAMU NOGUCHI
THAT ORIENTAL WAS REALLY ON TO SOMETHING!

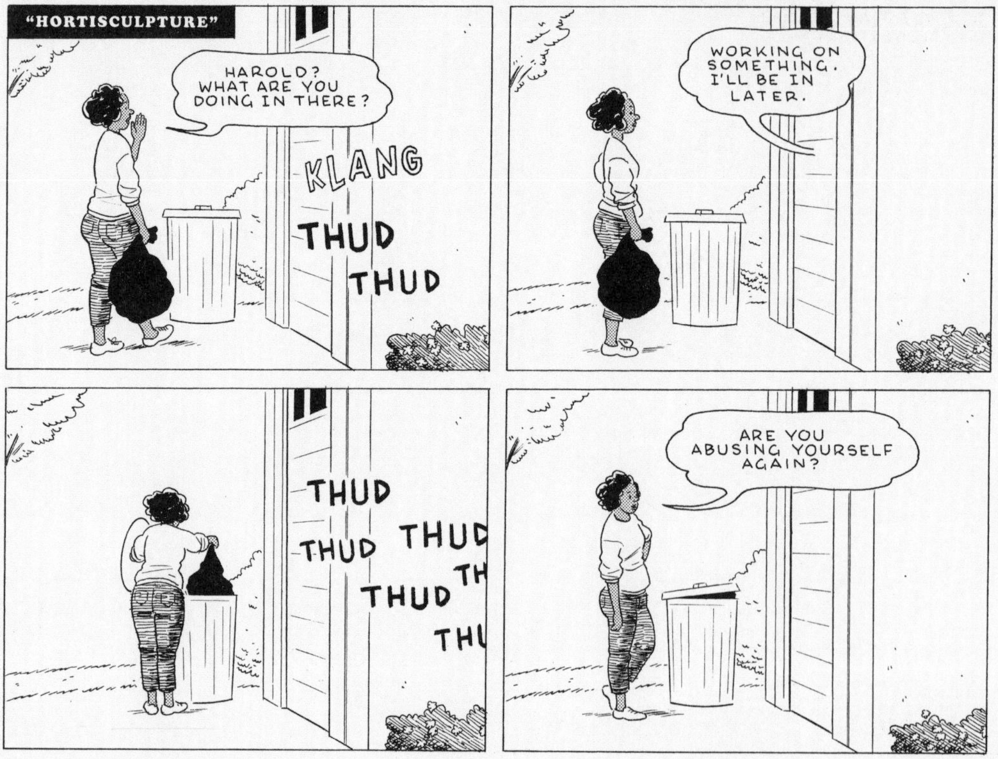
"HORTISCULPTURE"
HAROLD? WHAT ARE YOU DOING IN THERE?
KLANG
THUD
THUD
WORKING ON SOMETHING. I'LL BE IN LATER.
THUD
THUD THUD
THUD
ARE YOU ABUSING YOURSELF AGAIN?

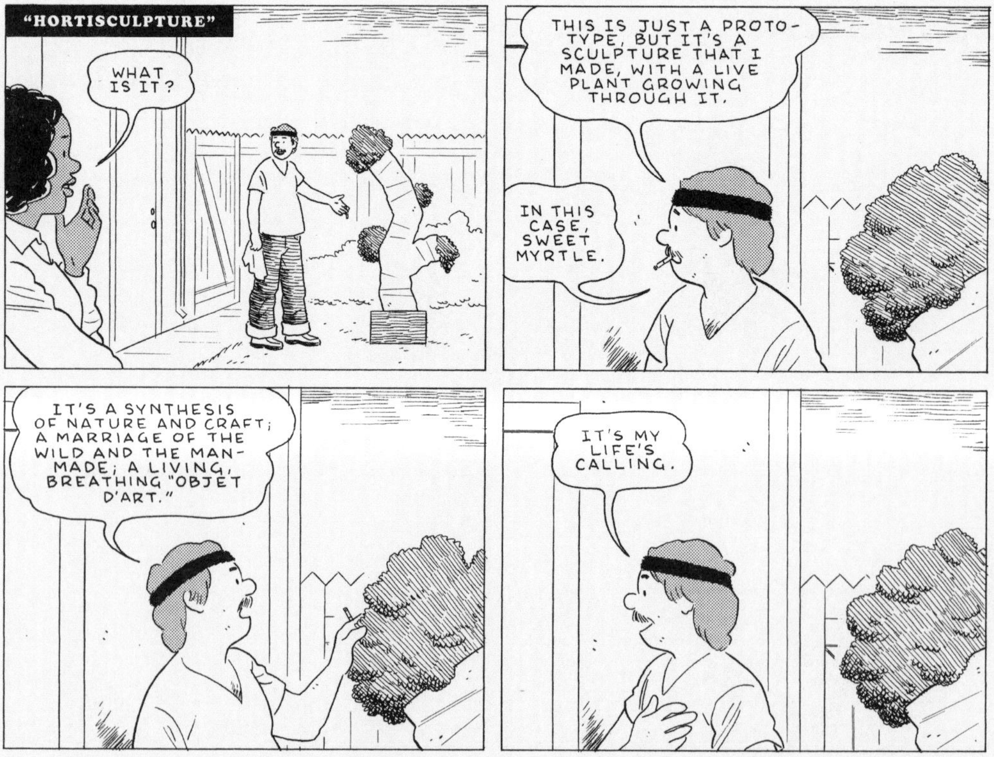
"HORTISCULPTURE"
WHAT IS IT?
THIS IS JUST A PROTOTYPE, BUT IT'S A SCULPTURE THAT I MADE, WITH A LIVE PLANT GROWING THROUGH IT.
IN THIS CASE, SWEET MYRTLE.
IT'S A SYNTHESIS OF NATURE AND CRAFT; A MARRIAGE OF THE WILD AND THE MAN-MADE; A LIVING, BREATHING "OBJET D'ART."
IT'S MY LIFE'S CALLING.

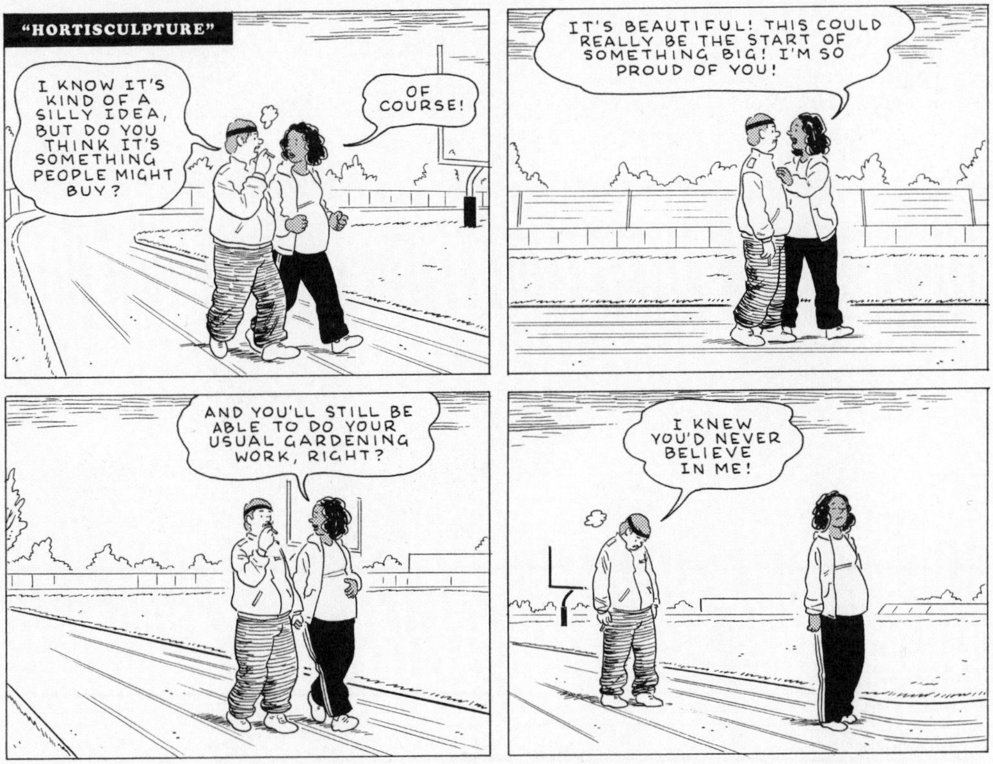
"HORTISCULPTURE"
I KNOW IT'S KIND OF A SILLY IDEA, BUT DO YOU THINK IT'S SOMETHING PEOPLE MIGHT BUY?
OF COURSE!
IT'S BEAUTIFUL! THIS COULD REALLY BE THE START OF SOMETHING BIG! I'M SO PROUD OF YOU!
AND YOU'LL STILL BE ABLE TO DO YOUR USUAL GARDENING WORK, RIGHT?
I KNEW YOU'D NEVER BELIEVE IN ME!

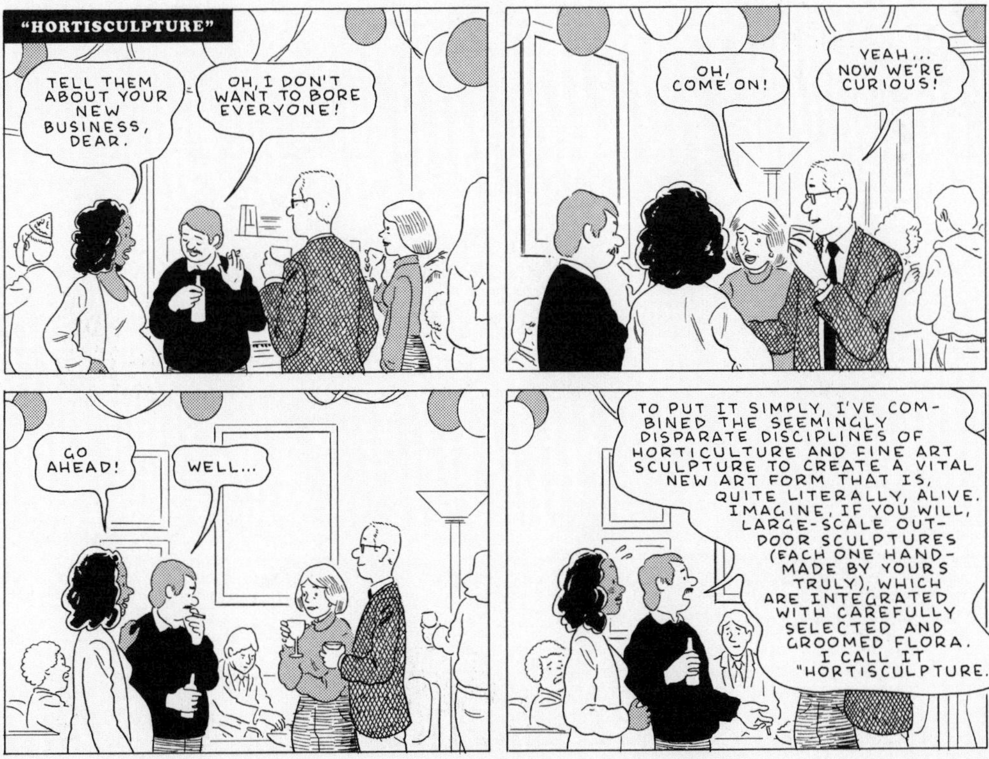
"HORTISCULPTURE"
TELL THEM ABOUT YOUR NEW BUSINESS, DEAR.
OH, I DON'T WANT TO BORE EVERYONE!
OH, COME ON!
YEAH... NOW WE'RE CURIOUS!
GO AHEAD!
WELL...
TO PUT IT SIMPLY, I'VE COMBINED THE SEEMINGLY DISPARATE DISCIPLINES OF HORTICULTURE AND FINE ART SCULPTURE TO CREATE A VITAL NEW ART FORM THAT IS, QUITE LITERALLY, ALIVE. IMAGINE, IF YOU WILL, LARGE-SCALE OUTDOOR SCULPTURES (EACH ONE HAND-MADE BY YOURS TRULY), WHICH ARE INTEGRATED WITH CAREFULLY SELECTED AND GROOMED FLORA. I CALL IT "HORTISCULPTURE."

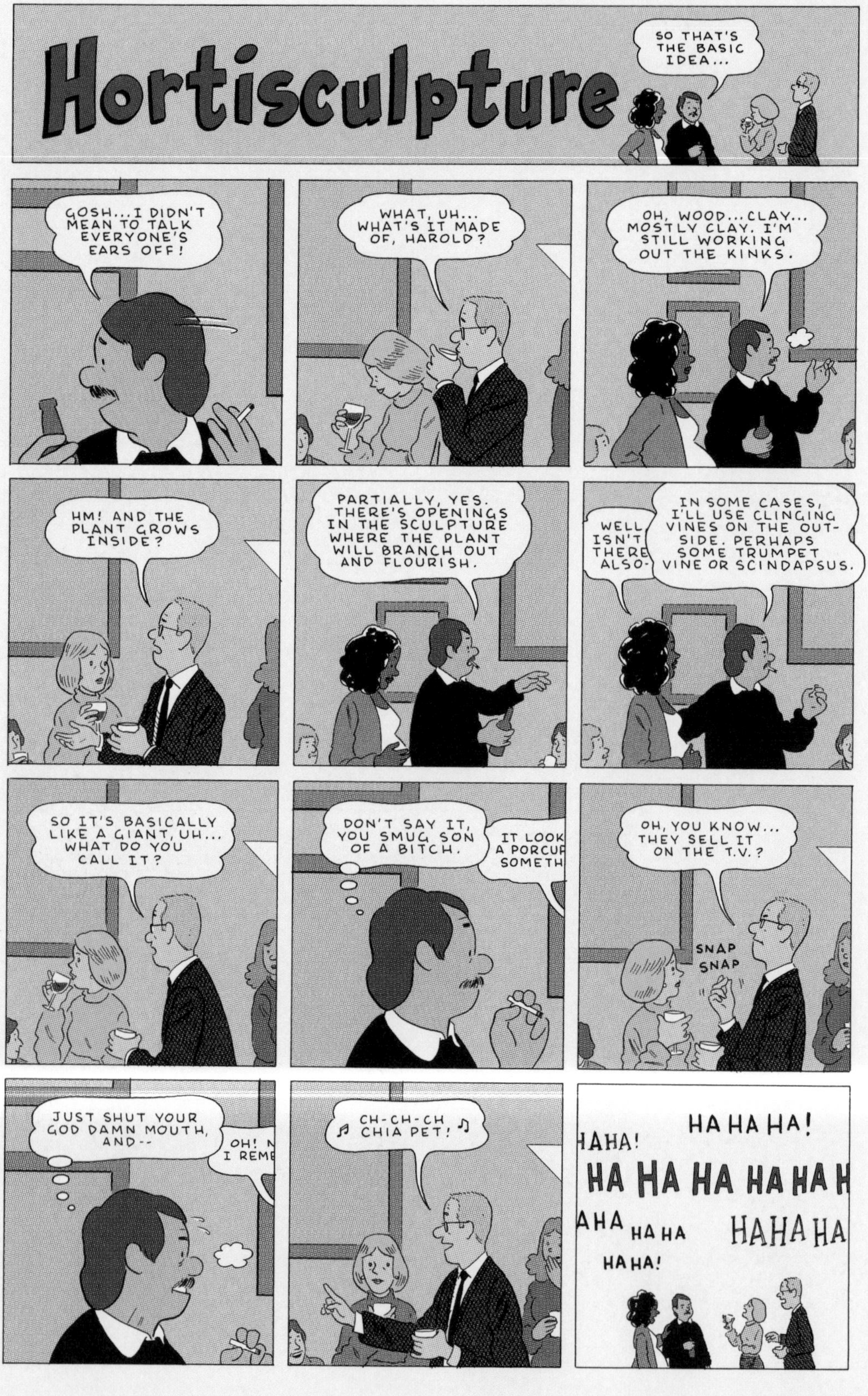
Hortisculpture
SO THAT'S THE BASIC IDEA...
GOSH...I DIDN'T MEAN TO TALK EVERYONE'S EARS OFF!
WHAT, UH... WHAT'S IT MADE OF, HAROLD?
OH, WOOD...CLAY... MOSTLY CLAY. I'M STILL WORKING OUT THE KINKS.
HM! AND THE PLANT GROWS INSIDE?
PARTIALLY, YES. THERE'S OPENINGS IN THE SCULPTURE WHERE THE PLANT WILL BRANCH OUT AND FLOURISH.
WELL ISN'T THERE ALSO-
IN SOME CASES, I'LL USE CLINGING VINES ON THE OUT-SIDE. PERHAPS SOME TRUMPET VINE OR SCINDAPSUS.
SO IT'S BASICALLY LIKE A GIANT, UH... WHAT DO YOU CALL IT?
DON'T SAY IT, YOU SMUG SON OF A BITCH.
IT LOOK A PORCUP SOMETH
OH, YOU KNOW... THEY SELL IT ON THE T.V.?
SNAP SNAP
JUST SHUT YOUR GOD DAMN MOUTH, AND--
OH! N I REME
CH-CH-CH CHIA PET!
HA HA HA!
HAHA!
HA HA HA HA HA HA H
AHA HA HA
HAHAHA
HA HA!

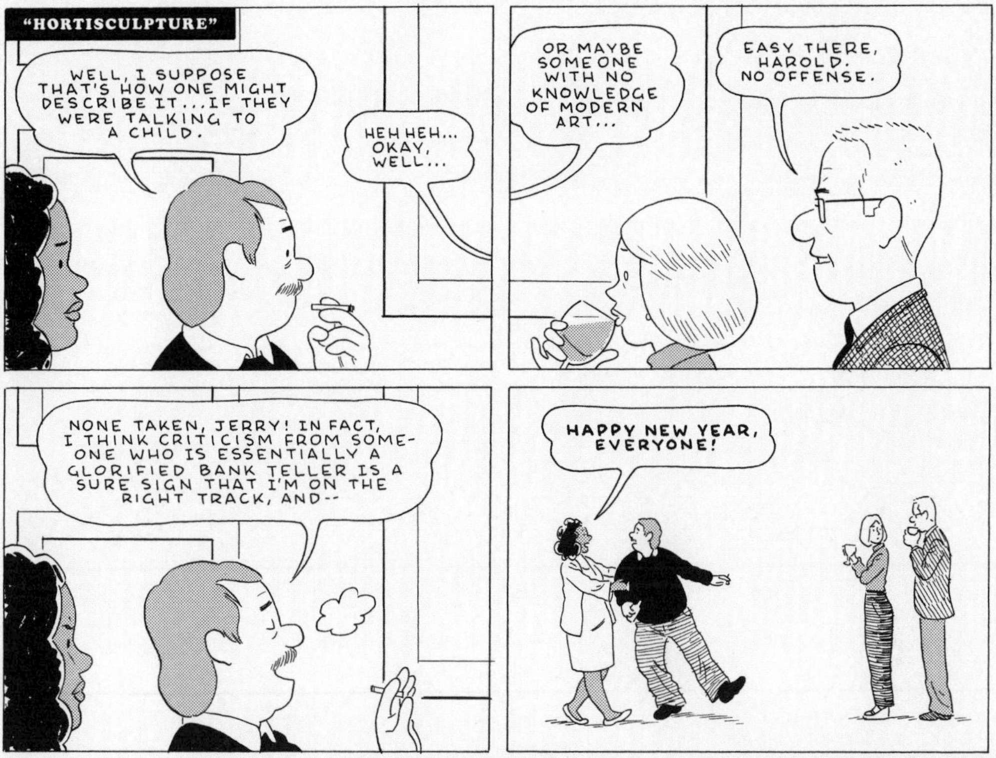
"HORTISCULPTURE"
WELL, I SUPPOSE THAT'S HOW ONE MIGHT DESCRIBE IT... IF THEY WERE TALKING TO A CHILD.
HEH HEH... OKAY, WELL...
OR MAYBE SOMEONE WITH NO KNOWLEDGE OF MODERN ART...
EASY THERE, HAROLD. NO OFFENSE.
NONE TAKEN, JERRY! IN FACT, I THINK CRITICISM FROM SOME-ONE WHO IS ESSENTIALLY A GLORIFIED BANK TELLER IS A SURE SIGN THAT I'M ON THE RIGHT TRACK, AND--
HAPPY NEW YEAR, EVERYONE!

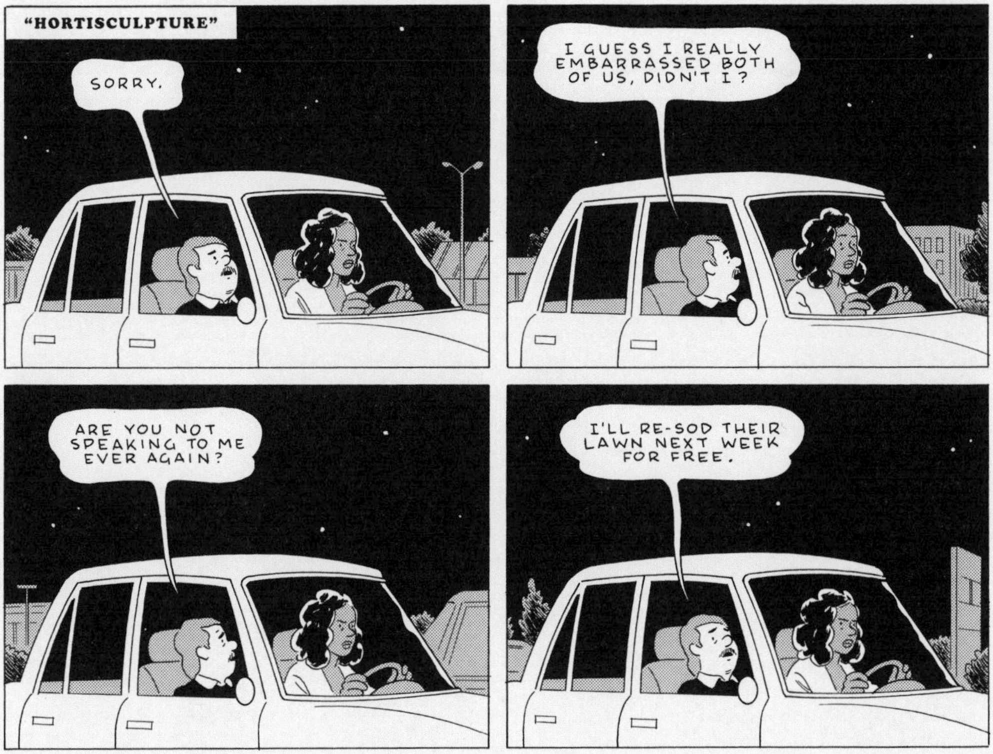
"HORTISCULPTURE"
SORRY.
I GUESS I REALLY EMBARRASSED BOTH OF US, DIDN'T I?
ARE YOU NOT SPEAKING TO ME EVER AGAIN?
I'LL RE-SOD THEIR LAWN NEXT WEEK FOR FREE.

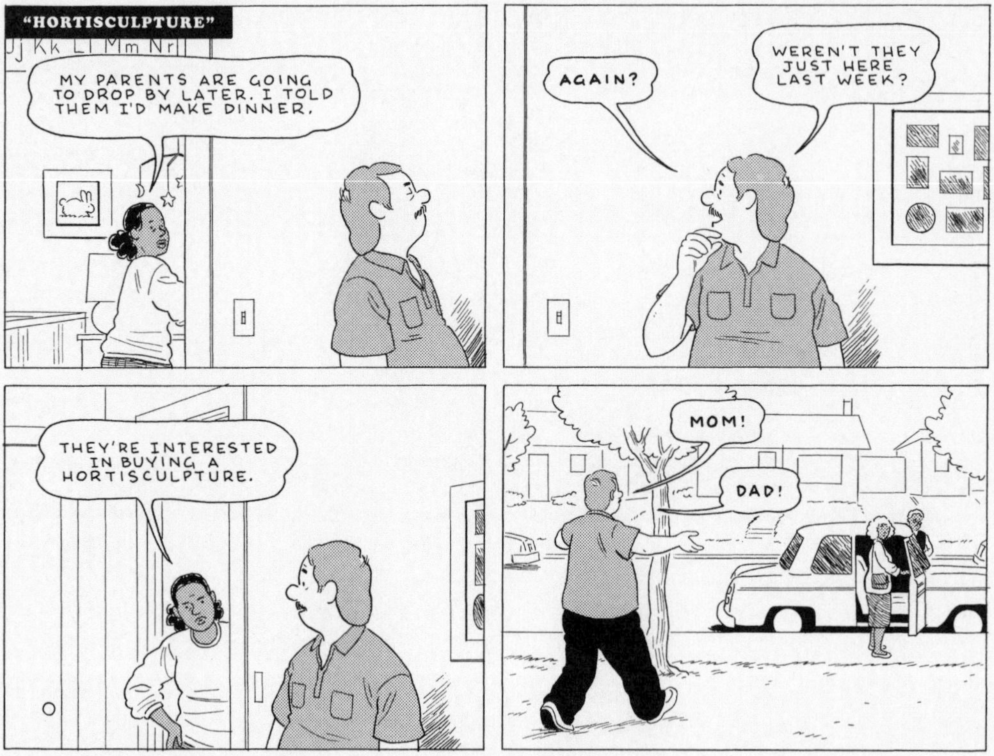
"HORTISCULPTURE"
MY PARENTS ARE GOING TO DROP BY LATER. I TOLD THEM I'D MAKE DINNER.
AGAIN?
WEREN'T THEY JUST HERE LAST WEEK?
THEY'RE INTERESTED IN BUYING A HORTISCULPTURE.
MOM!
DAD!

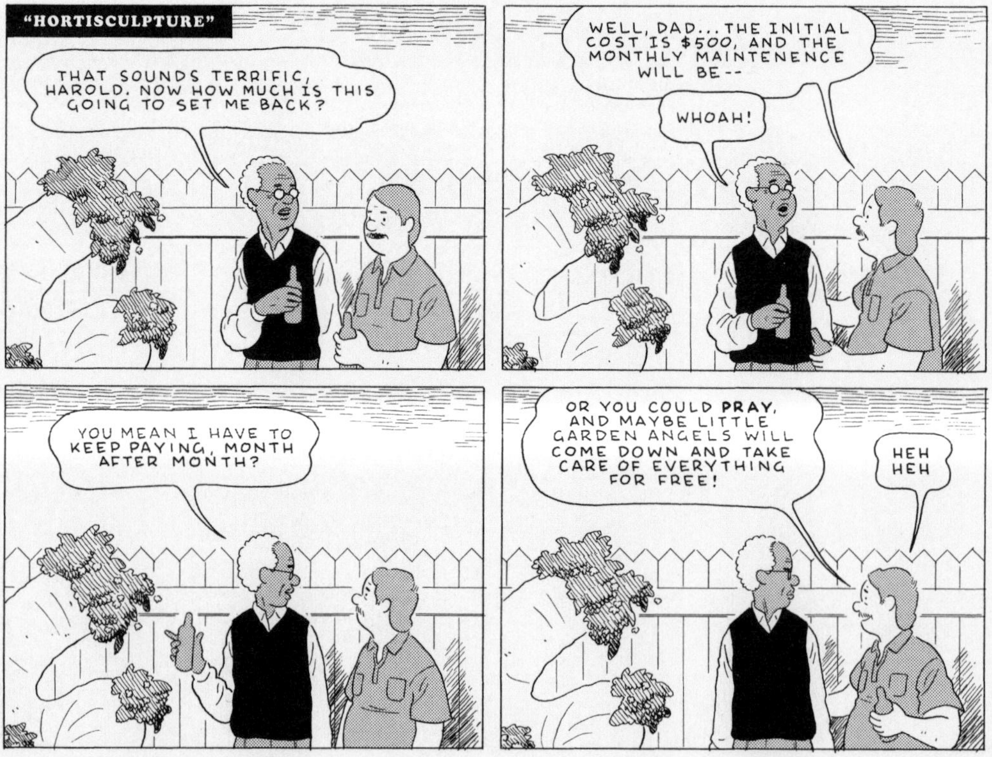
"HORTISCULPTURE"
THAT SOUNDS TERRIFIC, HAROLD. NOW HOW MUCH IS THIS GOING TO SET ME BACK?
WELL, DAD... THE INITIAL COST IS $500, AND THE MONTHLY MAINTENENCE WILL BE--
WHOAH!
YOU MEAN I HAVE TO KEEP PAYING, MONTH AFTER MONTH?
OR YOU COULD **PRAY**, AND MAYBE LITTLE GARDEN ANGELS WILL COME DOWN AND TAKE CARE OF EVERYTHING FOR FREE!
HEH HEH

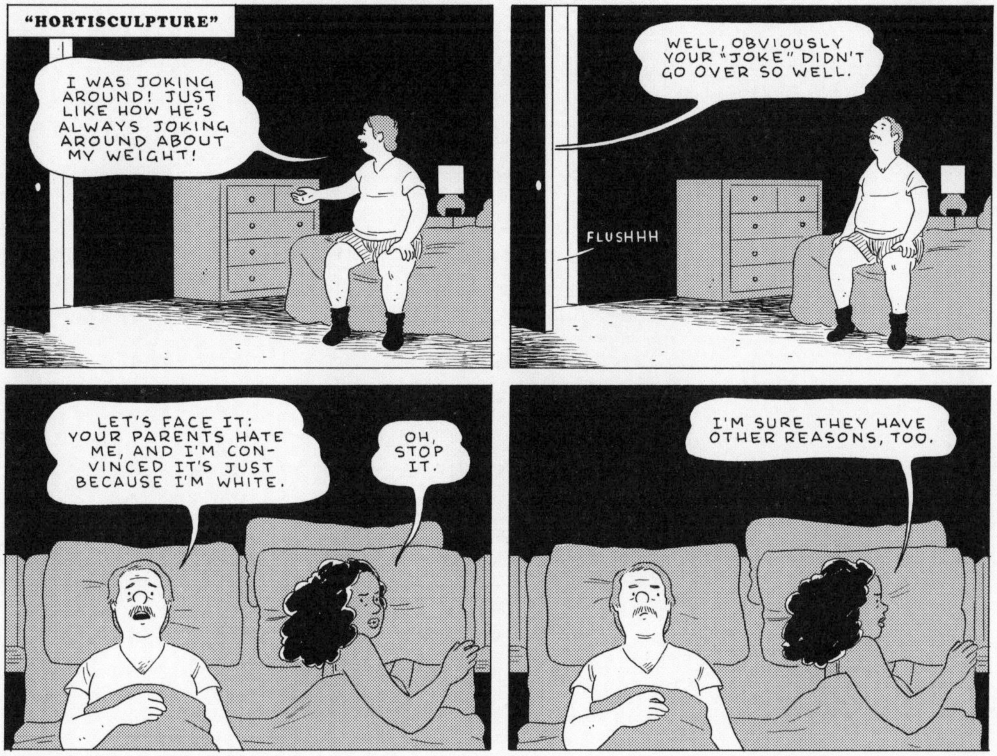
"HORTISCULPTURE"
I WAS JOKING AROUND! JUST LIKE HOW HE'S ALWAYS JOKING AROUND ABOUT MY WEIGHT!
WELL, OBVIOUSLY YOUR "JOKE" DIDN'T GO OVER SO WELL.
FLUSHHH
LET'S FACE IT: YOUR PARENTS HATE ME, AND I'M CONVINCED IT'S JUST BECAUSE I'M WHITE.
OH, STOP IT.
I'M SURE THEY HAVE OTHER REASONS, TOO.

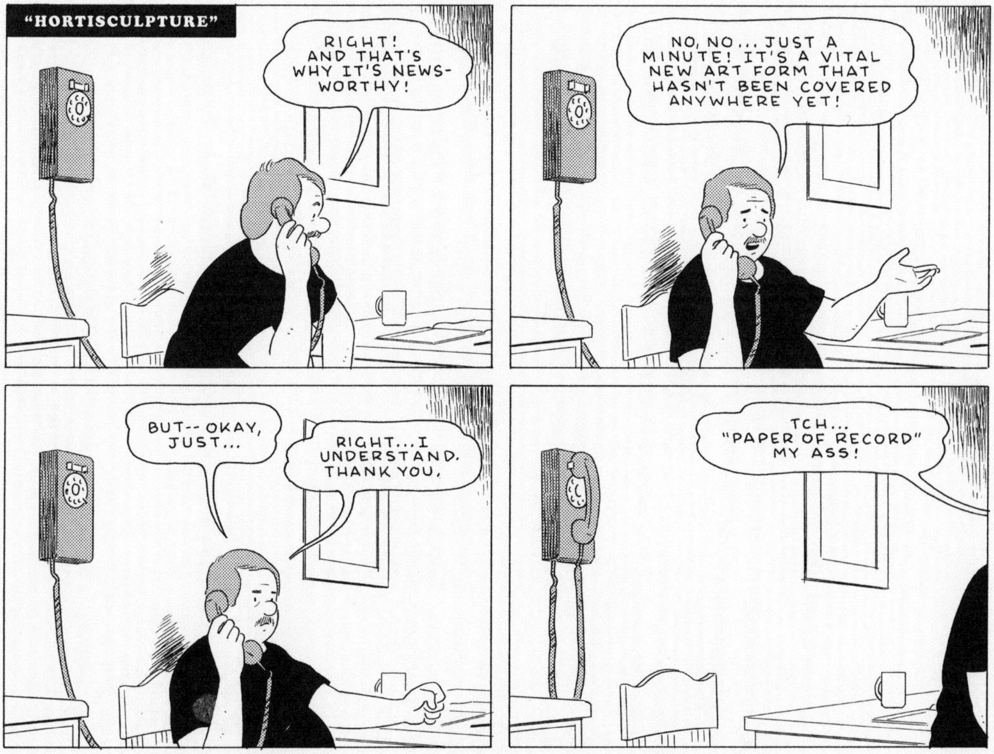
"HORTISCULPTURE"
RIGHT! AND THAT'S WHY IT'S NEWSWORTHY!
NO, NO... JUST A MINUTE! IT'S A VITAL NEW ART FORM THAT HASN'T BEEN COVERED ANYWHERE YET!
BUT--OKAY, JUST...
RIGHT...I UNDERSTAND. THANK YOU.
TCH... "PAPER OF RECORD" MY ASS!

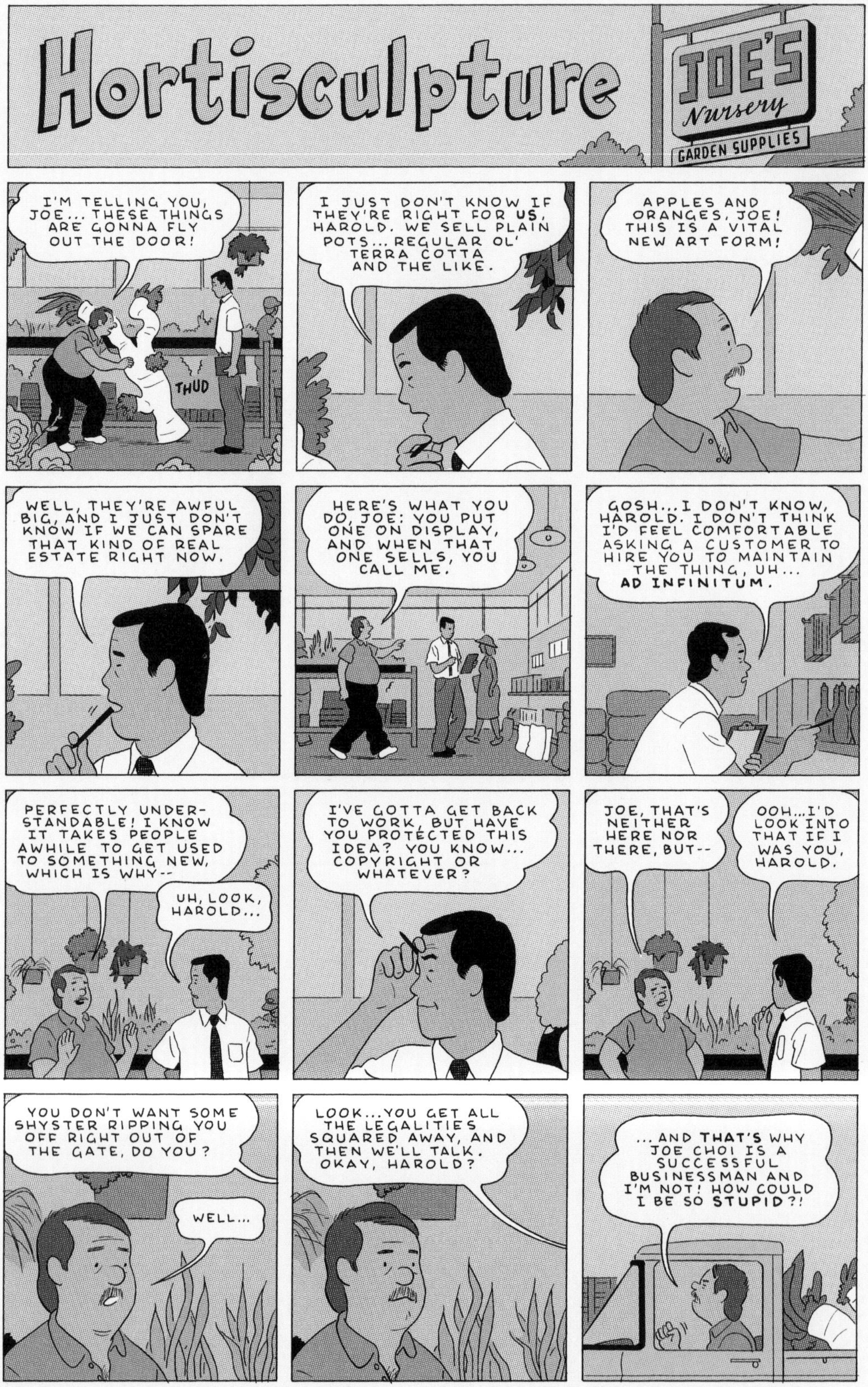
Hortisculpture
JOE'S Nursery
GARDEN SUPPLIES
I'M TELLING YOU, JOE... THESE THINGS ARE GONNA FLY OUT THE DOOR!
THUD
I JUST DON'T KNOW IF THEY'RE RIGHT FOR US, HAROLD. WE SELL PLAIN POTS... REGULAR OL' TERRA COTTA AND THE LIKE.
APPLES AND ORANGES, JOE! THIS IS A VITAL NEW ART FORM!
WELL, THEY'RE AWFUL BIG, AND I JUST DON'T KNOW IF WE CAN SPARE THAT KIND OF REAL ESTATE RIGHT NOW.
HERE'S WHAT YOU DO, JOE: YOU PUT ONE ON DISPLAY, AND WHEN THAT ONE SELLS, YOU CALL ME.
GOSH... I DON'T KNOW, HAROLD. I DON'T THINK I'D FEEL COMFORTABLE ASKING A CUSTOMER TO HIRE YOU TO MAINTAIN THE THING, UH... AD INFINITUM.
PERFECTLY UNDERSTANDABLE! I KNOW IT TAKES PEOPLE AWHILE TO GET USED TO SOMETHING NEW, WHICH IS WHY--
UH, LOOK, HAROLD...
I'VE GOTTA GET BACK TO WORK, BUT HAVE YOU PROTECTED THIS IDEA? YOU KNOW... COPYRIGHT OR WHATEVER?
JOE, THAT'S NEITHER HERE NOR THERE, BUT--
OOH... I'D LOOK INTO THAT IF I WAS YOU, HAROLD.
YOU DON'T WANT SOME SHYSTER RIPPING YOU OFF RIGHT OUT OF THE GATE, DO YOU?
WELL...
LOOK... YOU GET ALL THE LEGALITIES SQUARED AWAY, AND THEN WE'LL TALK. OKAY, HAROLD?
... AND THAT'S WHY JOE CHOI IS A SUCCESSFUL BUSINESSMAN AND I'M NOT! HOW COULD I BE SO STUPID?!

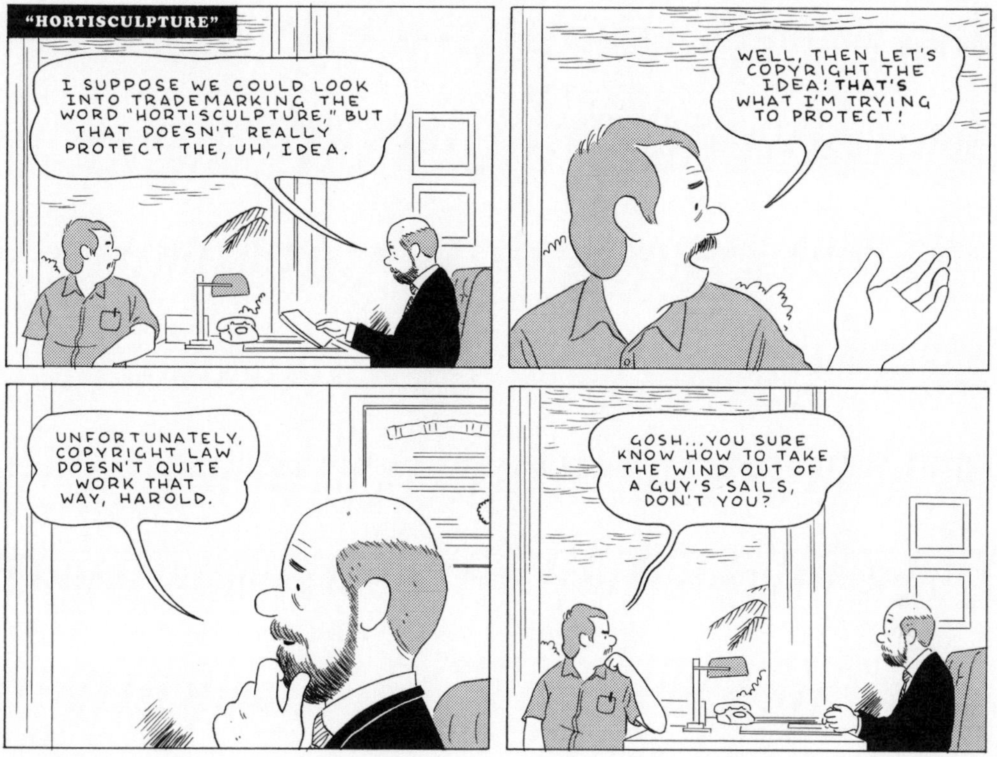
"HORTISCULPTURE"
I SUPPOSE WE COULD LOOK INTO TRADEMARKING THE WORD "HORTISCULPTURE," BUT THAT DOESN'T REALLY PROTECT THE, UH, IDEA.
WELL, THEN LET'S COPYRIGHT THE IDEA! **THAT'S** WHAT I'M TRYING TO PROTECT!
UNFORTUNATELY, COPYRIGHT LAW DOESN'T QUITE WORK THAT WAY, HAROLD.
GOSH... YOU SURE KNOW HOW TO TAKE THE WIND OUT OF A GUY'S SAILS, DON'T YOU?

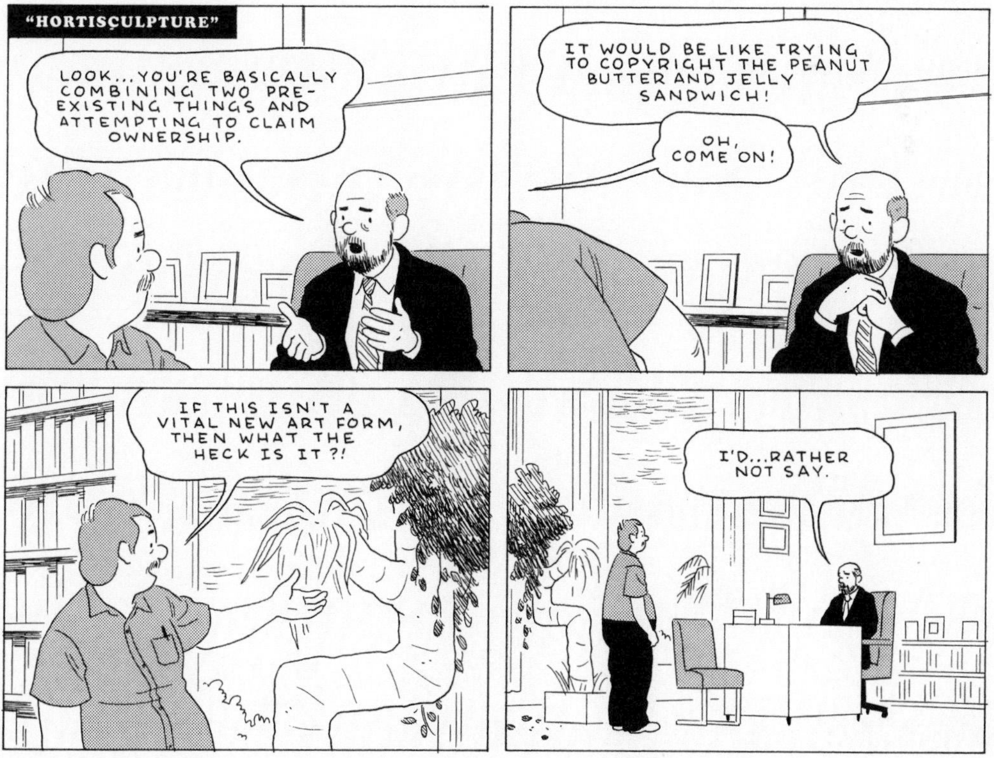
"HORTISCULPTURE"
LOOK... YOU'RE BASICALLY COMBINING TWO PRE-EXISTING THINGS AND ATTEMPTING TO CLAIM OWNERSHIP.
IT WOULD BE LIKE TRYING TO COPYRIGHT THE PEANUT BUTTER AND JELLY SANDWICH!
OH, COME ON!
IF THIS ISN'T A VITAL NEW ART FORM, THEN WHAT THE HECK IS IT?!
I'D... RATHER NOT SAY.

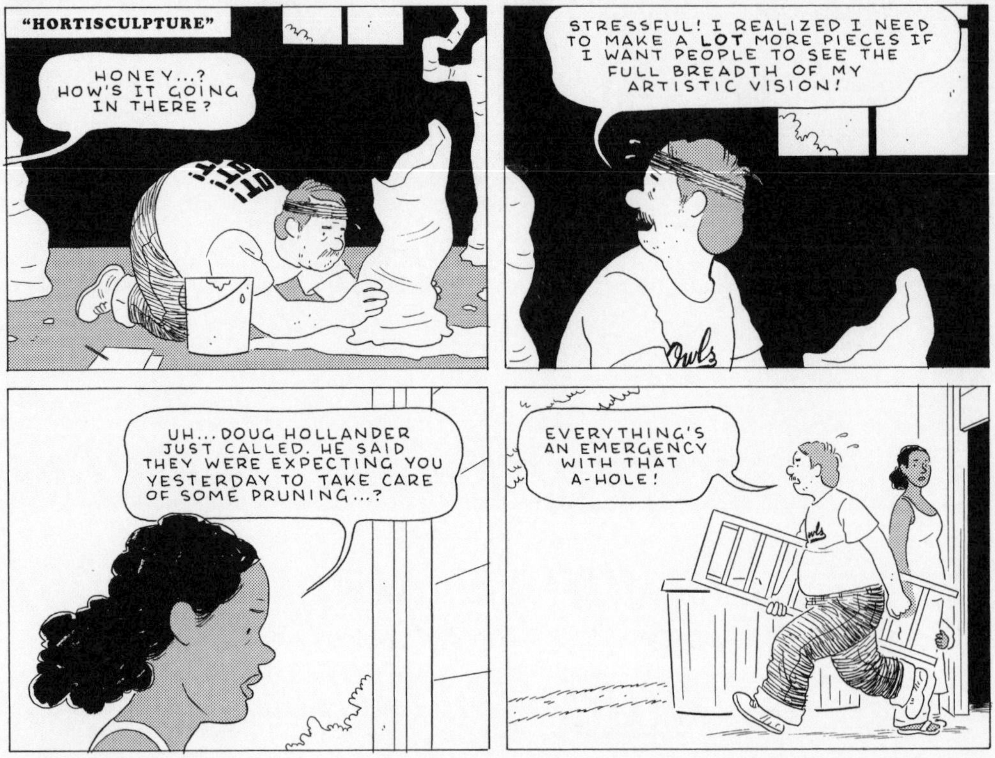
"HORTISCULPTURE"
HONEY...? HOW'S IT GOING IN THERE?
STRESSFUL! I REALIZED I NEED TO MAKE A **LOT** MORE PIECES IF I WANT PEOPLE TO SEE THE FULL BREADTH OF MY ARTISTIC VISION!
UH... DOUG HOLLANDER JUST CALLED. HE SAID THEY WERE EXPECTING YOU YESTERDAY TO TAKE CARE OF SOME PRUNING...?
EVERYTHING'S AN EMERGENCY WITH THAT A-HOLE!

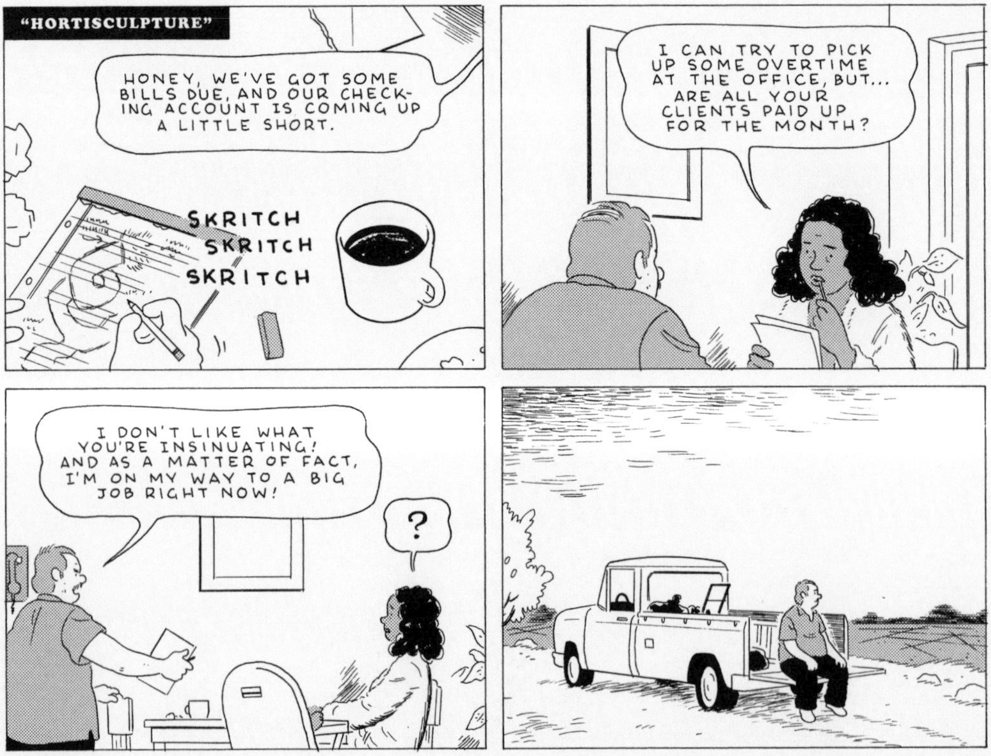
"HORTISCULPTURE"
HONEY, WE'VE GOT SOME BILLS DUE, AND OUR CHECKING ACCOUNT IS COMING UP A LITTLE SHORT.
SKRITCH
SKRITCH
SKRITCH
I CAN TRY TO PICK UP SOME OVERTIME AT THE OFFICE, BUT... ARE ALL YOUR CLIENTS PAID UP FOR THE MONTH?
I DON'T LIKE WHAT YOU'RE INSINUATING! AND AS A MATTER OF FACT, I'M ON MY WAY TO A BIG JOB RIGHT NOW!
?

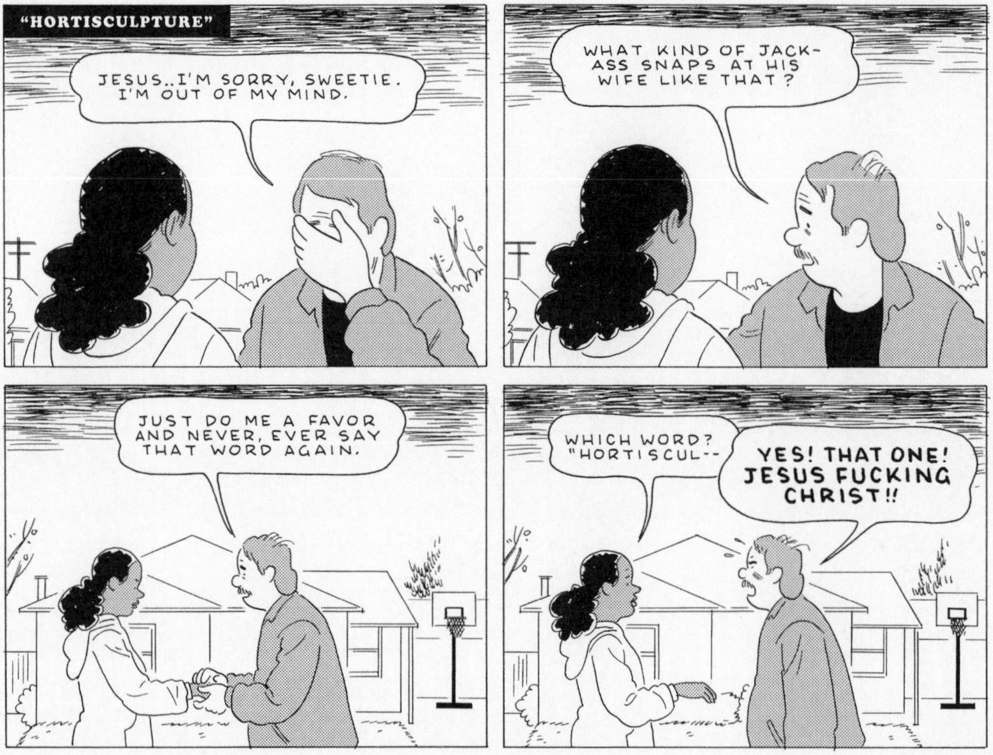
"HORTISCULPTURE"
JESUS.. I'M SORRY, SWEETIE. I'M OUT OF MY MIND.
WHAT KIND OF JACK-ASS SNAPS AT HIS WIFE LIKE THAT?
JUST DO ME A FAVOR AND NEVER, EVER SAY THAT WORD AGAIN.
WHICH WORD? "HORTISCUL--
YES! THAT ONE! JESUS FUCKING CHRIST!!

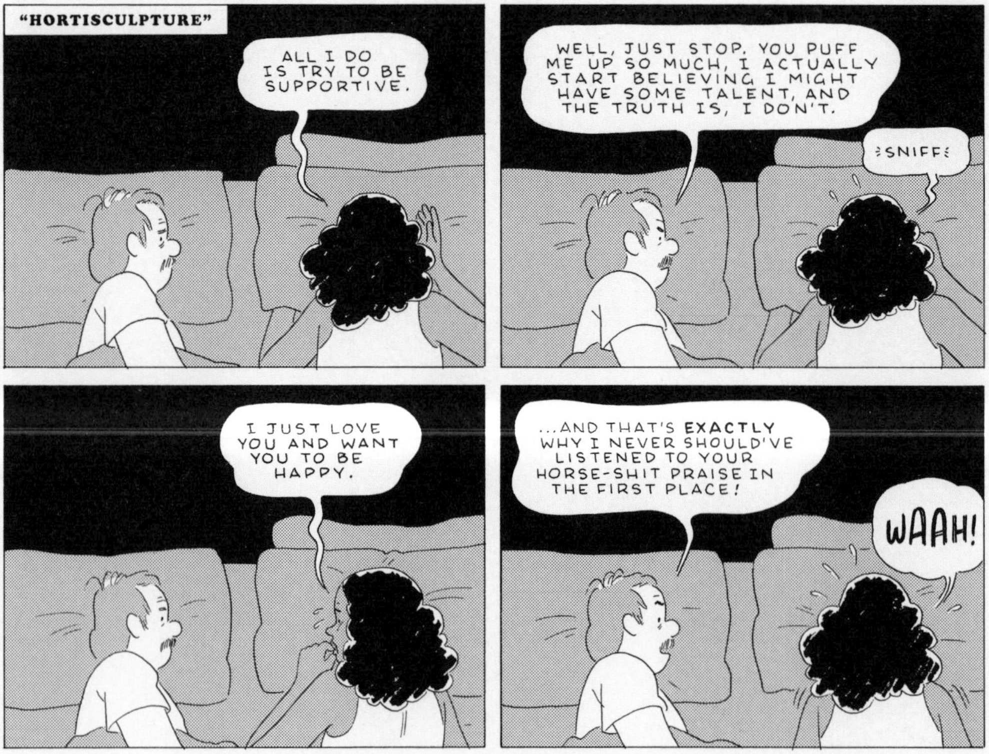
"HORTISCULPTURE"
ALL I DO IS TRY TO BE SUPPORTIVE.
WELL, JUST STOP. YOU PUFF ME UP SO MUCH, I ACTUALLY START BELIEVING I MIGHT HAVE SOME TALENT, AND THE TRUTH IS, I DON'T.
SNIFF
I JUST LOVE YOU AND WANT YOU TO BE HAPPY.
...AND THAT'S EXACTLY WHY I NEVER SHOULD'VE LISTENED TO YOUR HORSE-SHIT PRAISE IN THE FIRST PLACE!
WAAH!

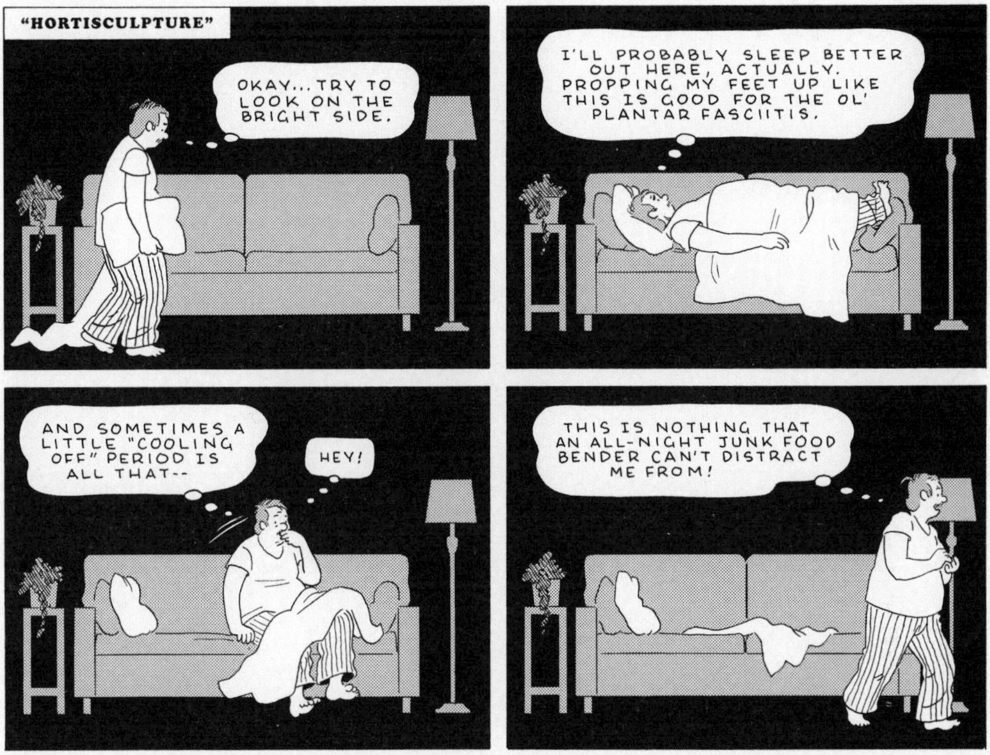
"HORTISCULPTURE"
OKAY... TRY TO LOOK ON THE BRIGHT SIDE.
I'LL PROBABLY SLEEP BETTER OUT HERE, ACTUALLY. PROPPING MY FEET UP LIKE THIS IS GOOD FOR THE OL' PLANTAR FASCIITIS.
AND SOMETIMES A LITTLE "COOLING OFF" PERIOD IS ALL THAT--
HEY!
THIS IS NOTHING THAT AN ALL-NIGHT JUNK FOOD BENDER CAN'T DISTRACT ME FROM!

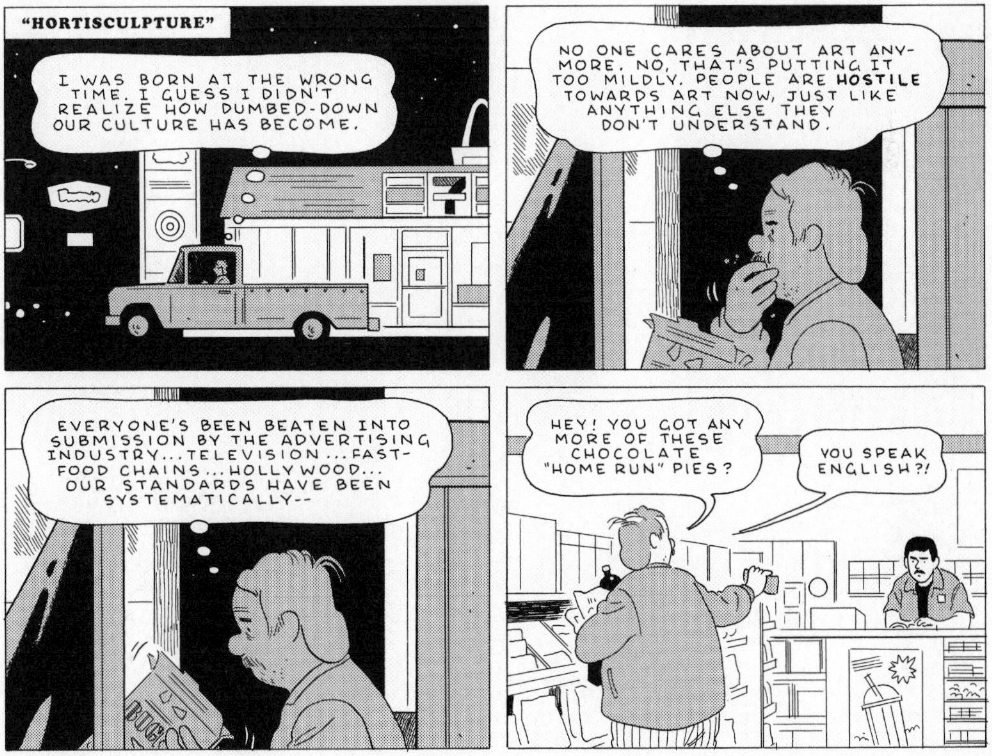
"HORTISCULPTURE"
I WAS BORN AT THE WRONG TIME. I GUESS I DIDN'T REALIZE HOW DUMBED-DOWN OUR CULTURE HAS BECOME.
NO ONE CARES ABOUT ART ANYMORE. NO, THAT'S PUTTING IT TOO MILDLY. PEOPLE ARE **HOSTILE** TOWARDS ART NOW, JUST LIKE ANYTHING ELSE THEY DON'T UNDERSTAND.
EVERYONE'S BEEN BEATEN INTO SUBMISSION BY THE ADVERTISING INDUSTRY... TELEVISION... FAST-FOOD CHAINS... HOLLYWOOD... OUR STANDARDS HAVE BEEN SYSTEMATICALLY--
HEY! YOU GOT ANY MORE OF THESE CHOCOLATE "HOME RUN" PIES?
YOU SPEAK ENGLISH?!

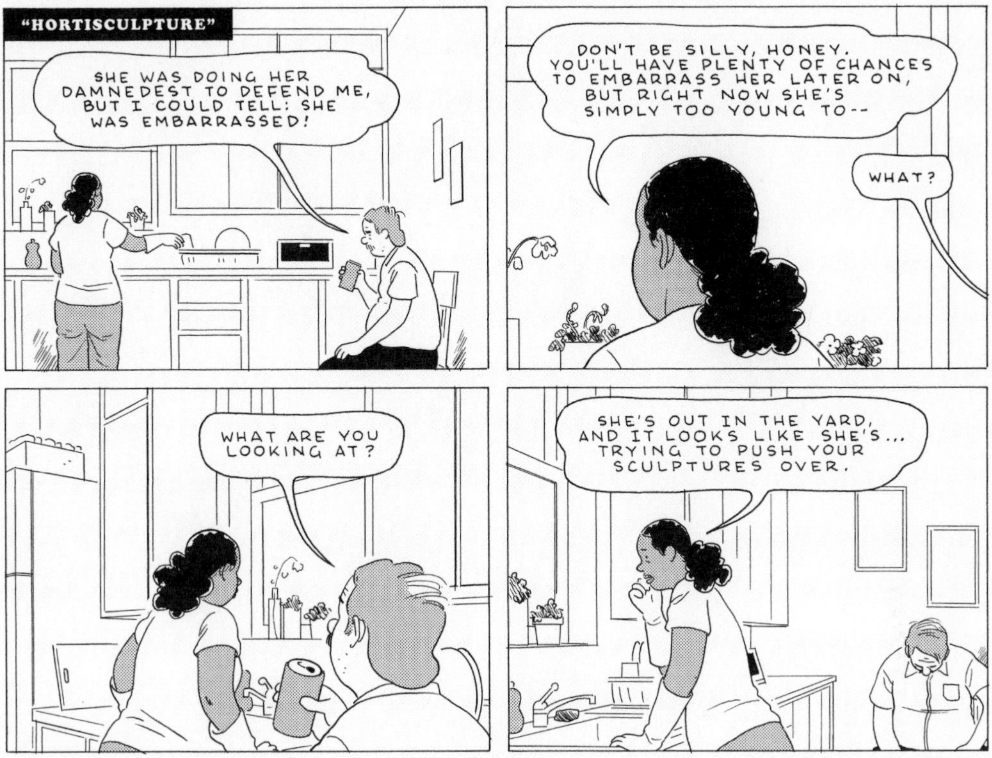
"HORTISCULPTURE"
SHE WAS DOING HER DAMNEDEST TO DEFEND ME, BUT I COULD TELL: SHE WAS EMBARRASSED!
DON'T BE SILLY, HONEY. YOU'LL HAVE PLENTY OF CHANCES TO EMBARRASS HER LATER ON, BUT RIGHT NOW SHE'S SIMPLY TOO YOUNG TO--
WHAT?
WHAT ARE YOU LOOKING AT?
SHE'S OUT IN THE YARD, AND IT LOOKS LIKE SHE'S... TRYING TO PUSH YOUR SCULPTURES OVER.

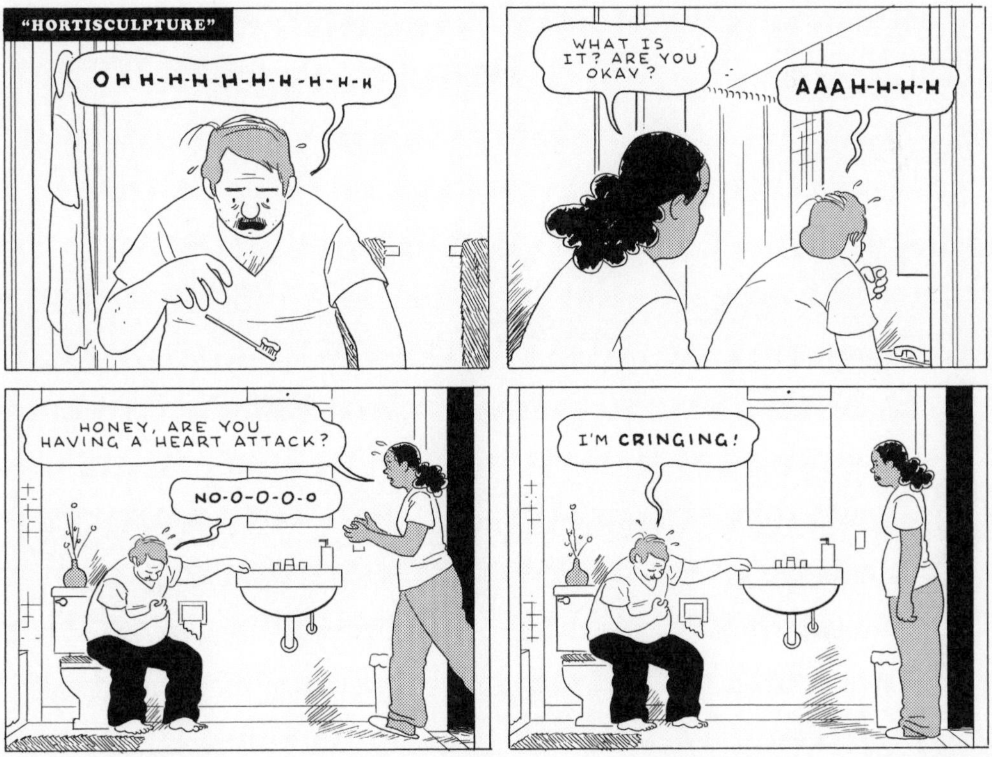
"HORTISCULPTURE"
OHH-H-H-H-H-H-H-H-H
WHAT IS IT? ARE YOU OKAY?
AAAH-H-H-H
HONEY, ARE YOU HAVING A HEART ATTACK?
NO-O-O-O-O
I'M CRINGING!

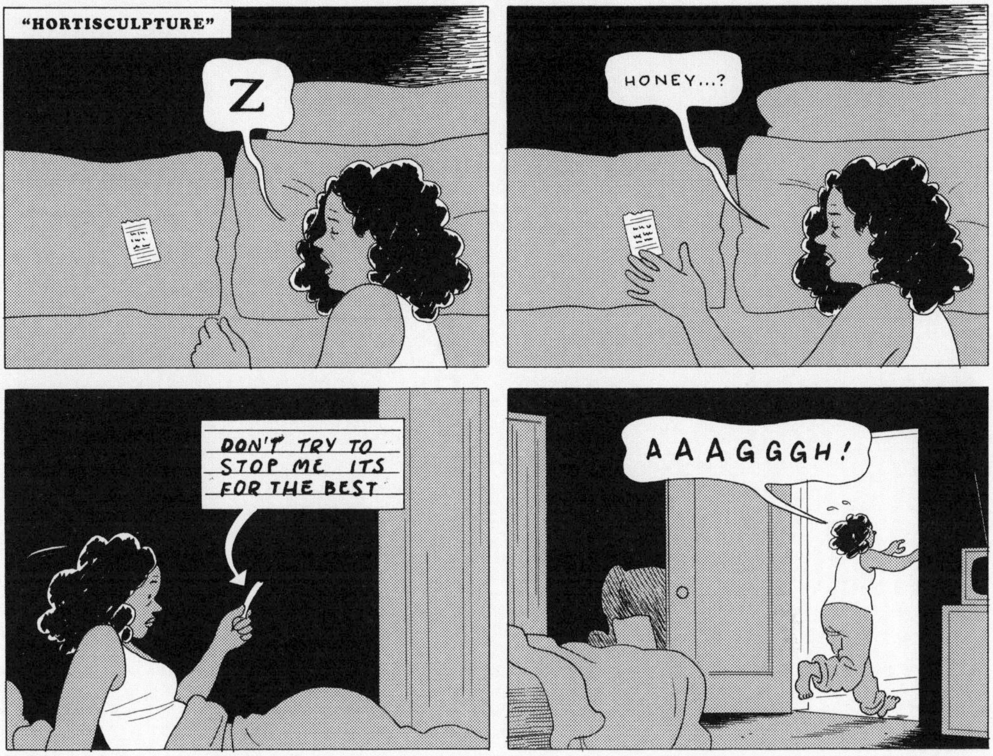
"HORTISCULPTURE"
Z
HONEY...?
DON'T TRY TO STOP ME ITS FOR THE BEST
AAAGGGH!

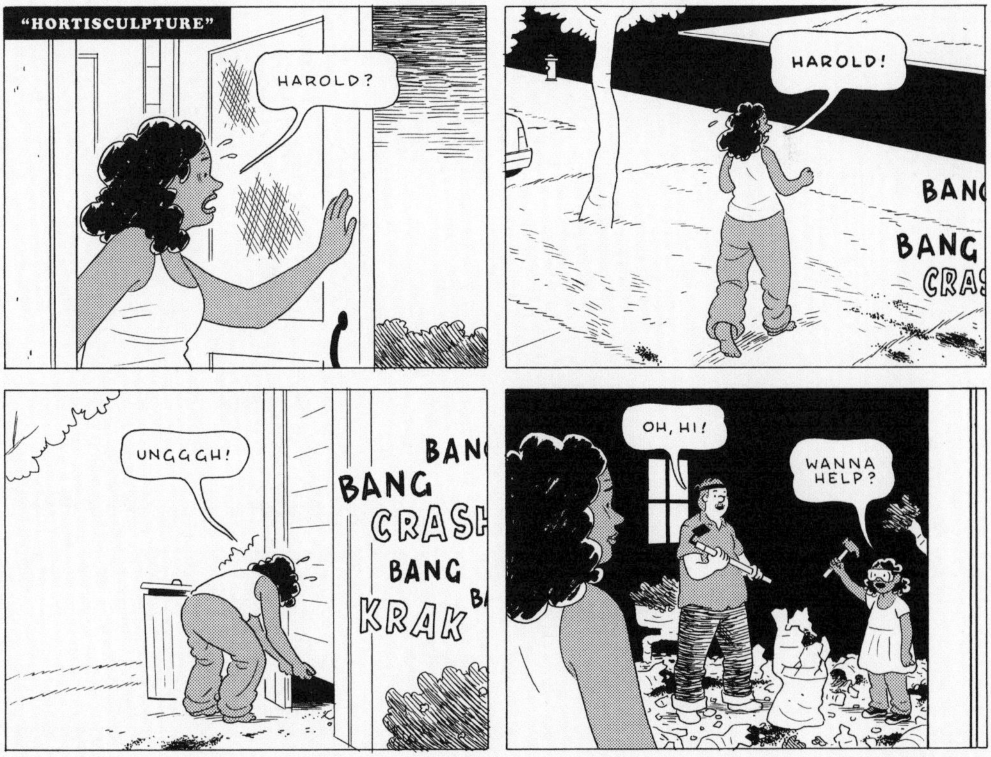
"HORTISCULPTURE"
HAROLD?
HAROLD!
BAN
BANG
CRAS
UNGGGH!
BAN
BANG
CRASH
BANG
KRAK
OH, HI!
WANNA HELP?

AMBER SWEET

AMBER SWEET

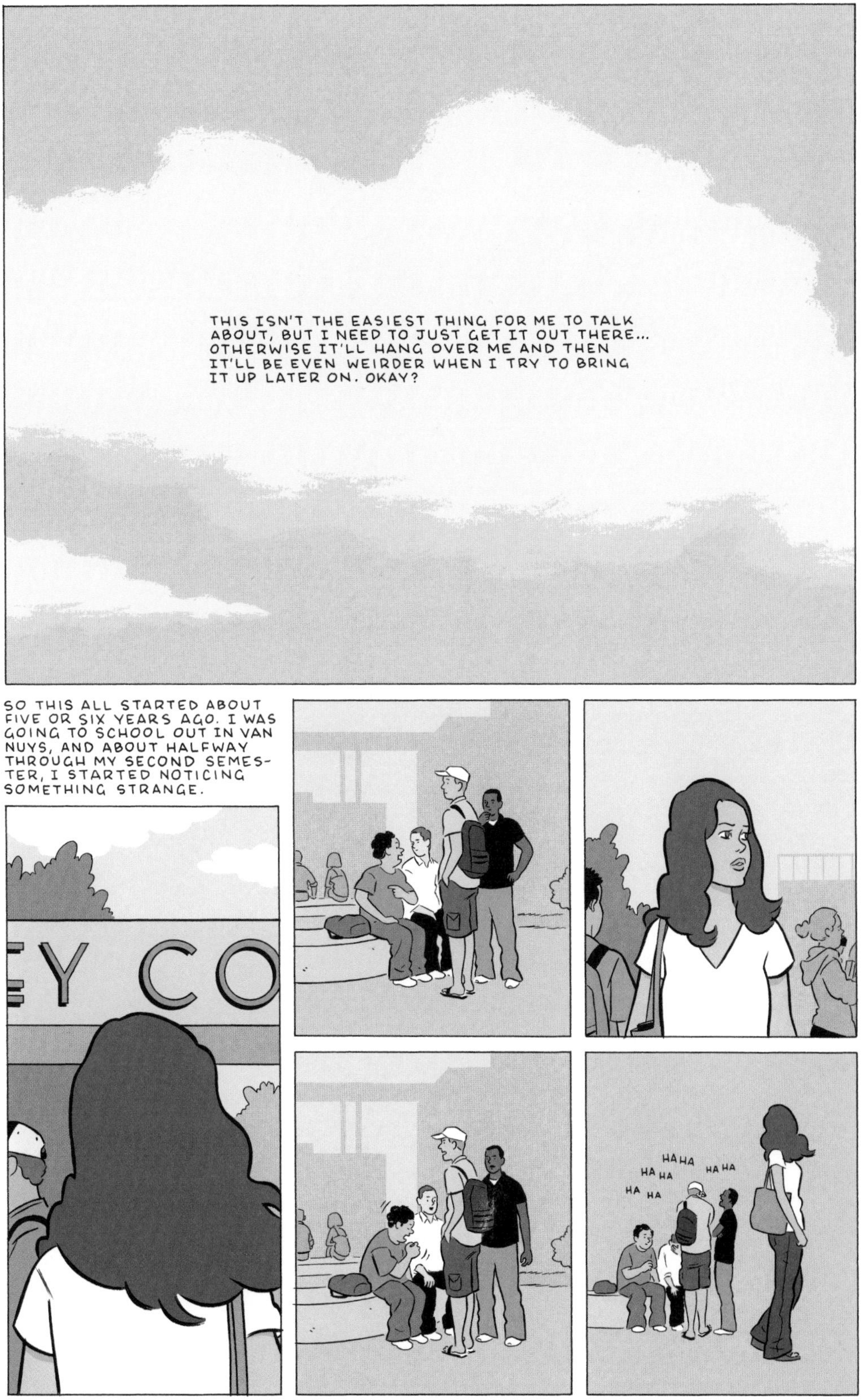
THIS ISN'T THE EASIEST THING FOR ME TO TALK ABOUT, BUT I NEED TO JUST GET IT OUT THERE... OTHERWISE IT'LL HANG OVER ME AND THEN IT'LL BE EVEN WEIRDER WHEN I TRY TO BRING IT UP LATER ON. OKAY?
SO THIS ALL STARTED ABOUT FIVE OR SIX YEARS AGO. I WAS GOING TO SCHOOL OUT IN VAN NUYS, AND ABOUT HALFWAY THROUGH MY SECOND SEMESTER, I STARTED NOTICING SOMETHING STRANGE.
EY CO
HA HA
HA HA
HA HA
HA HA

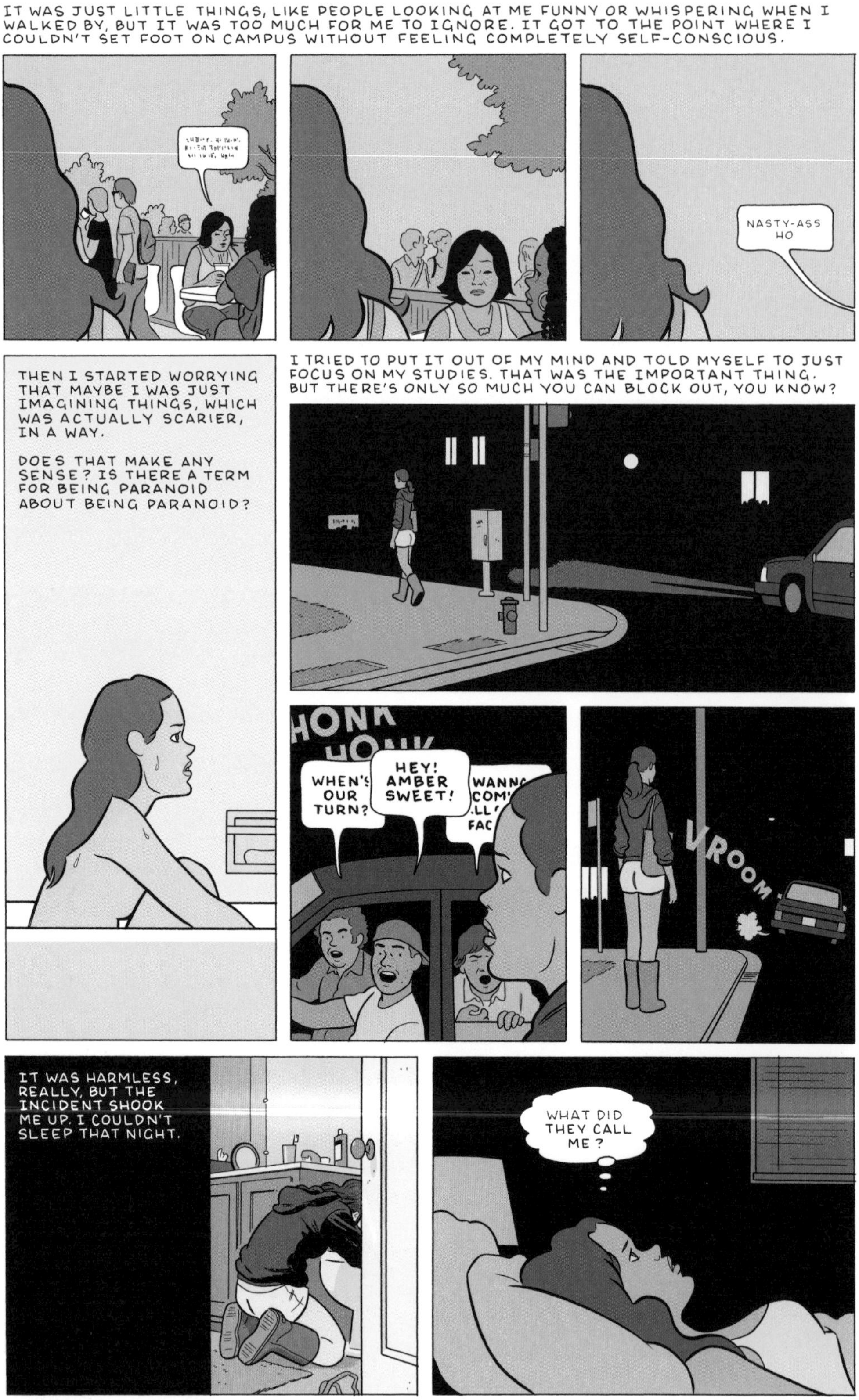
IT WAS JUST LITTLE THINGS, LIKE PEOPLE LOOKING AT ME FUNNY OR WHISPERING WHEN I WALKED BY, BUT IT WAS TOO MUCH FOR ME TO IGNORE. IT GOT TO THE POINT WHERE I COULDN'T SET FOOT ON CAMPUS WITHOUT FEELING COMPLETELY SELF-CONSCIOUS.
NASTY-ASS HO
THEN I STARTED WORRYING THAT MAYBE I WAS JUST IMAGINING THINGS, WHICH WAS ACTUALLY SCARIER, IN A WAY.
DOES THAT MAKE ANY SENSE? IS THERE A TERM FOR BEING PARANOID ABOUT BEING PARANOID?
I TRIED TO PUT IT OUT OF MY MIND AND TOLD MYSELF TO JUST FOCUS ON MY STUDIES. THAT WAS THE IMPORTANT THING. BUT THERE'S ONLY SO MUCH YOU CAN BLOCK OUT, YOU KNOW?
HONK
HONK
WHEN'S OUR TURN?
HEY! AMBER SWEET!
VROOM
IT WAS HARMLESS, REALLY, BUT THE INCIDENT SHOOK ME UP. I COULDN'T SLEEP THAT NIGHT.
WHAT DID THEY CALL ME?

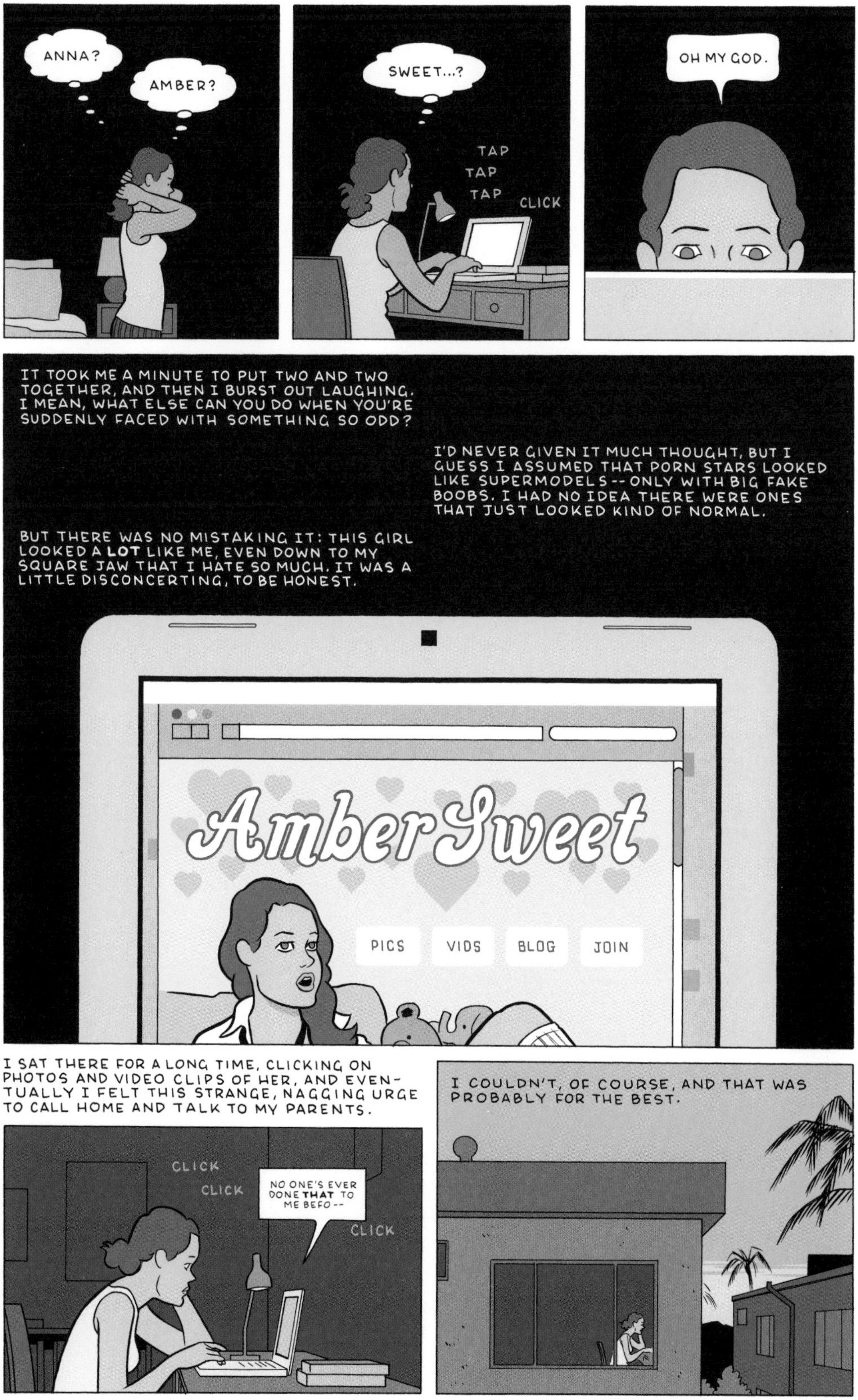
ANNA?
AMBER?
SWEET...?
TAP
TAP
TAP
CLICK
OH MY GOD.
IT TOOK ME A MINUTE TO PUT TWO AND TWO TOGETHER, AND THEN I BURST OUT LAUGHING. I MEAN, WHAT ELSE CAN YOU DO WHEN YOU'RE SUDDENLY FACED WITH SOMETHING SO ODD?
I'D NEVER GIVEN IT MUCH THOUGHT, BUT I GUESS I ASSUMED THAT PORN STARS LOOKED LIKE SUPERMODELS -- ONLY WITH BIG FAKE BOOBS. I HAD NO IDEA THERE WERE ONES THAT JUST LOOKED KIND OF NORMAL.
BUT THERE WAS NO MISTAKING IT: THIS GIRL LOOKED A **LOT** LIKE ME, EVEN DOWN TO MY SQUARE JAW THAT I HATE SO MUCH. IT WAS A LITTLE DISCONCERTING, TO BE HONEST.
AmberSweet
PICS
VIDS
BLOG
JOIN
I SAT THERE FOR A LONG TIME, CLICKING ON PHOTOS AND VIDEO CLIPS OF HER, AND EVENTUALLY I FELT THIS STRANGE, NAGGING URGE TO CALL HOME AND TALK TO MY PARENTS.
CLICK
CLICK
NO ONE'S EVER DONE **THAT** TO ME BEFO--
CLICK
I COULDN'T, OF COURSE, AND THAT WAS PROBABLY FOR THE BEST.

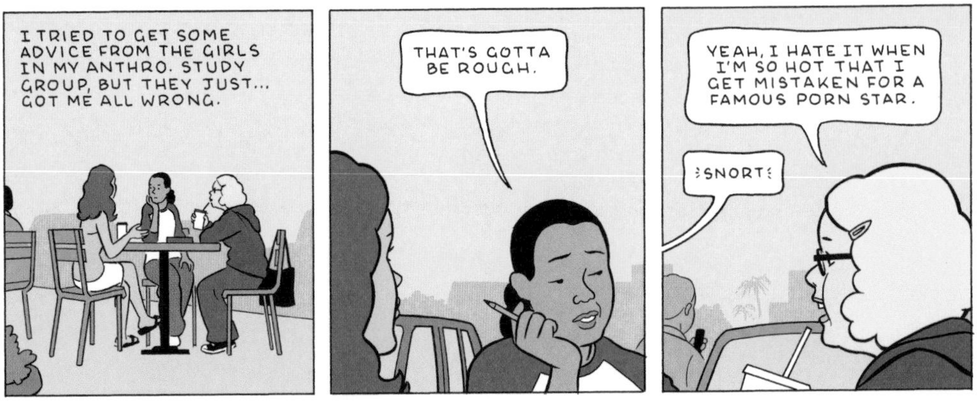
I TRIED TO GET SOME ADVICE FROM THE GIRLS IN MY ANTHRO. STUDY GROUP, BUT THEY JUST... GOT ME ALL WRONG.
THAT'S GOTTA BE ROUGH.
YEAH, I HATE IT WHEN I'M SO HOT THAT I GET MISTAKEN FOR A FAMOUS PORN STAR.
SNORT

AROUND THIS TIME A GUY FROM MY PSYCH. CLASS ASKED ME OUT. HE WASN'T REALLY MY TYPE PHYSICALLY, BUT HE SEEMED KIND OF SMART AND FUNNY, AND MORE IMPORTANTLY, OBLIVIOUS TO THE STUPID CAMPUS GOSSIP.

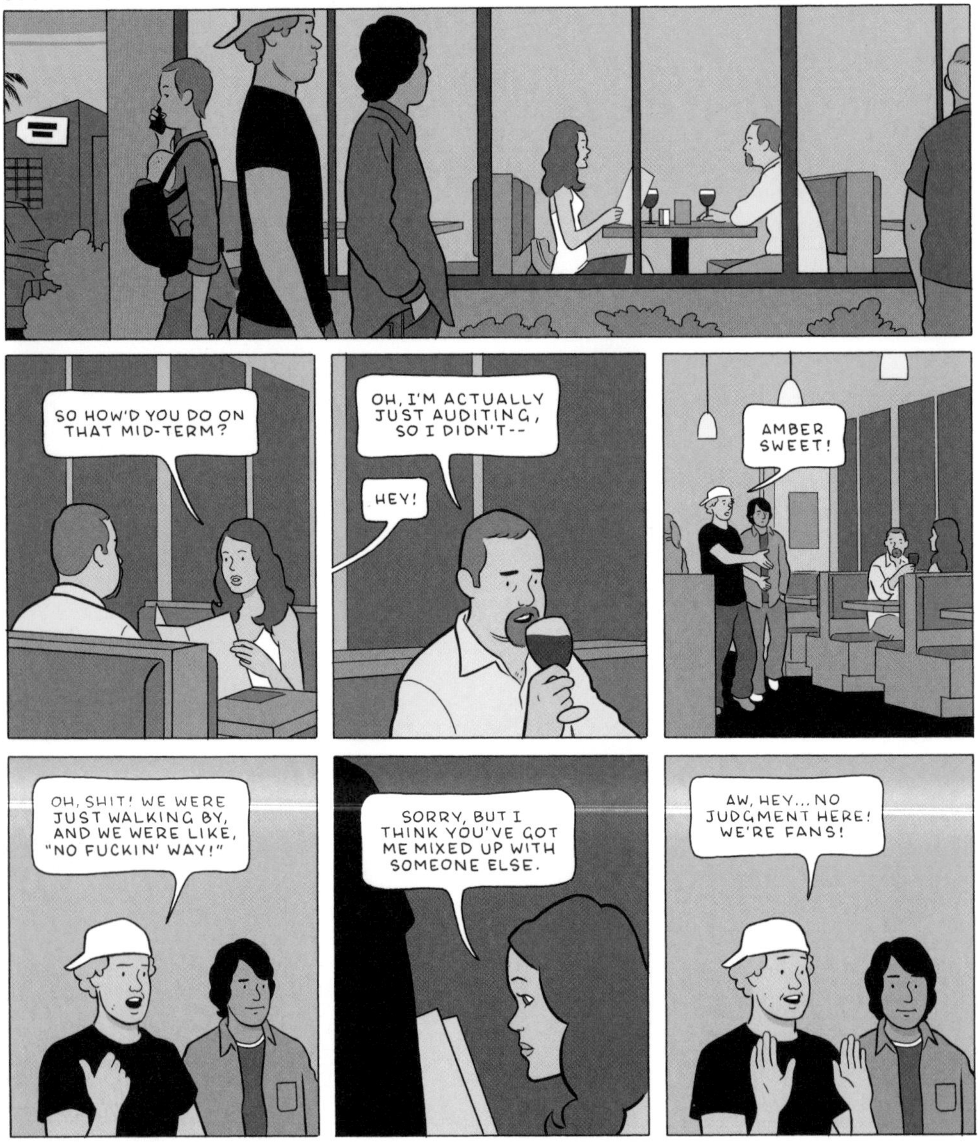
SO HOW'D YOU DO ON THAT MID-TERM?
OH, I'M ACTUALLY JUST AUDITING, SO I DIDN'T--
HEY!
AMBER SWEET!
OH, SHIT! WE WERE JUST WALKING BY, AND WE WERE LIKE, "NO FUCKIN' WAY!"
SORRY, BUT I THINK YOU'VE GOT ME MIXED UP WITH SOMEONE ELSE.
AW, HEY... NO JUDGMENT HERE! WE'RE FANS!

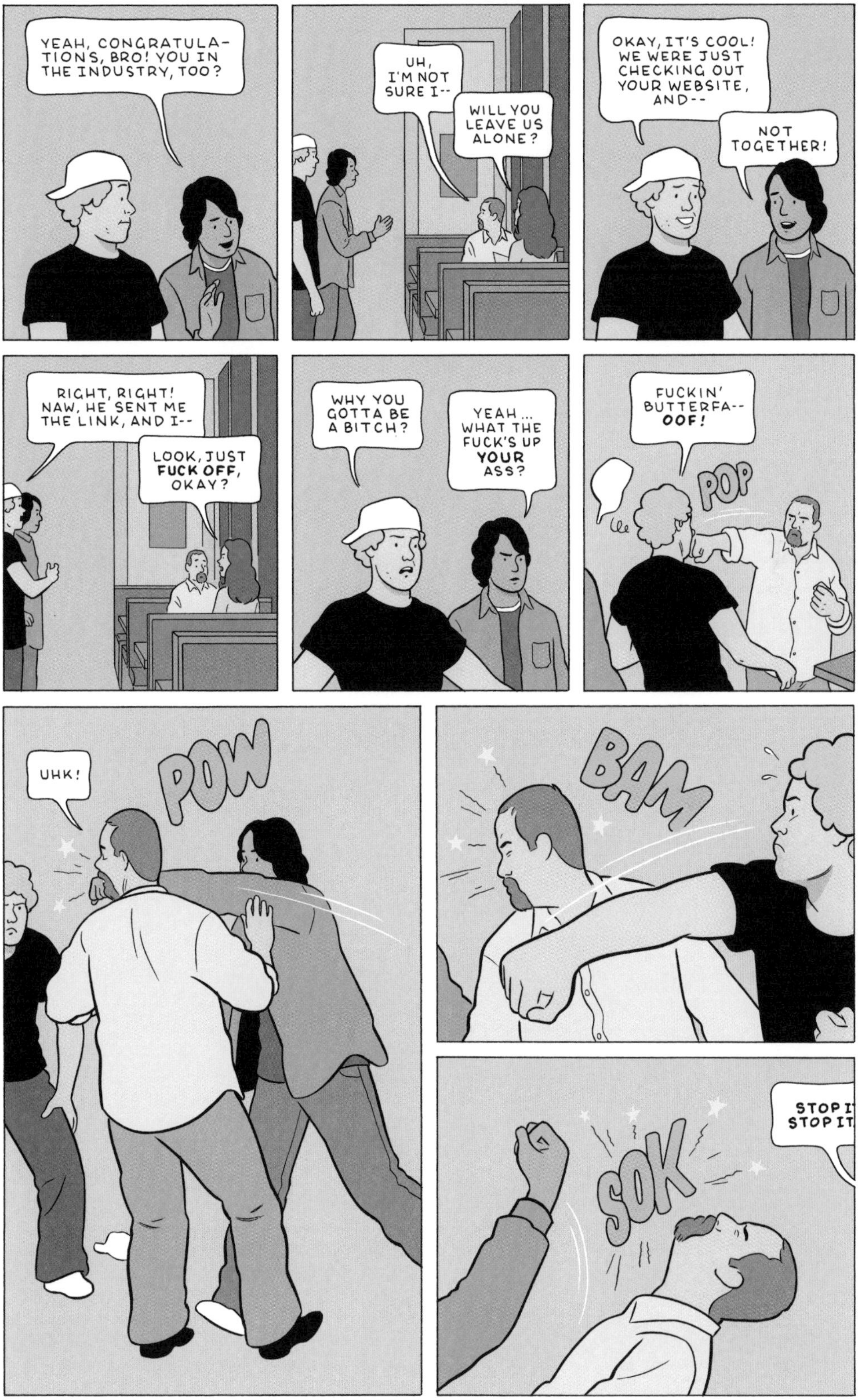

YEAH, CONGRATULATIONS, BRO! YOU IN THE INDUSTRY, TOO?
UH, I'M NOT SURE I--
WILL YOU LEAVE US ALONE?
OKAY, IT'S COOL! WE WERE JUST CHECKING OUT YOUR WEBSITE, AND--
NOT TOGETHER!
RIGHT, RIGHT! NAW, HE SENT ME THE LINK, AND I--
LOOK, JUST **FUCK OFF**, OKAY?
WHY YOU GOTTA BE A BITCH?
YEAH... WHAT THE FUCK'S UP **YOUR** ASS?
FUCKIN' BUTTERFA-- **OOF!**
POP
UHK!
POW
BAM
SOK
STOP IT
STOP IT

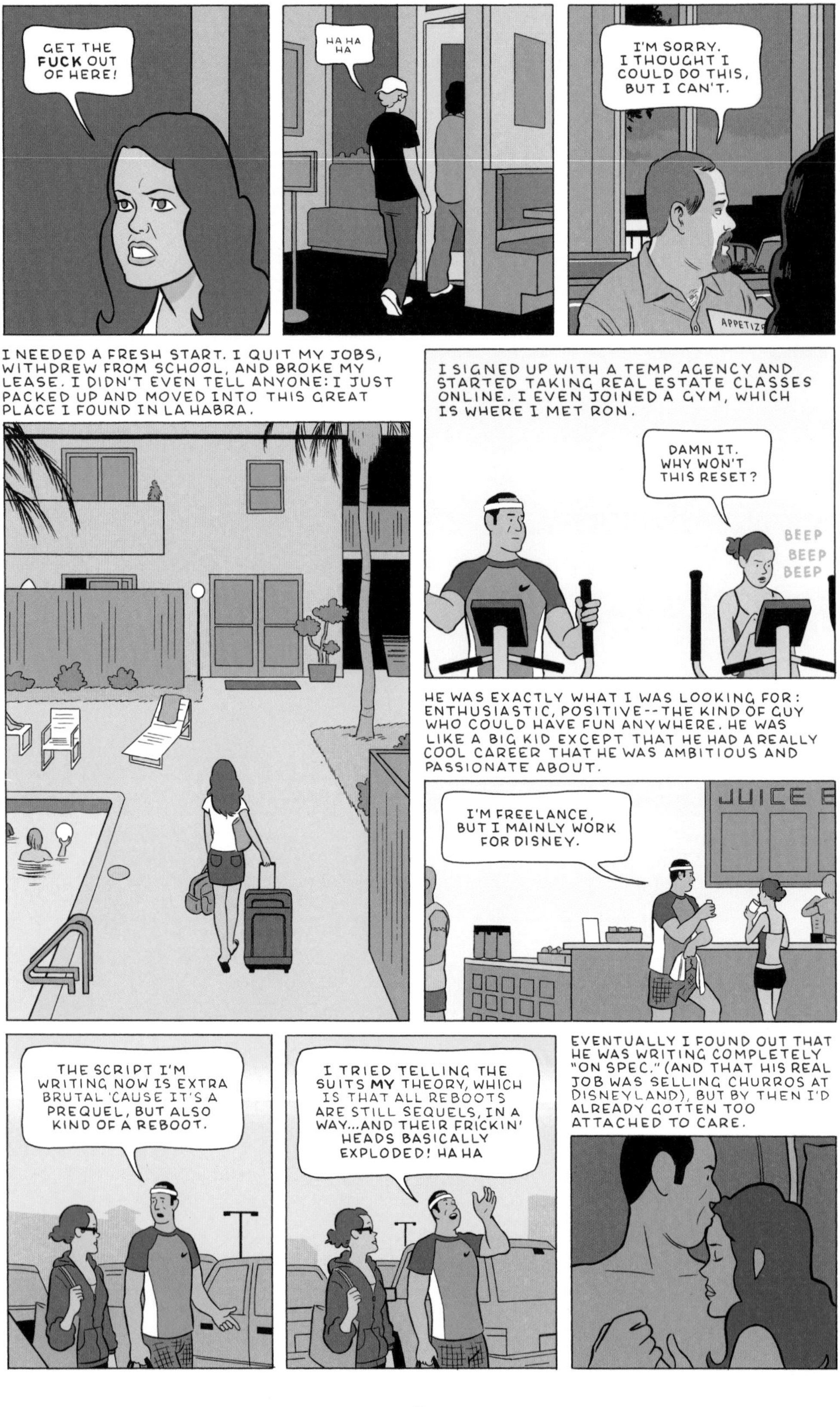

GET THE **FUCK** OUT OF HERE!
HA HA HA
I'M SORRY. I THOUGHT I COULD DO THIS, BUT I CAN'T.
APPETIZ
I NEEDED A FRESH START. I QUIT MY JOBS, WITHDREW FROM SCHOOL, AND BROKE MY LEASE. I DIDN'T EVEN TELL ANYONE: I JUST PACKED UP AND MOVED INTO THIS GREAT PLACE I FOUND IN LA HABRA.
I SIGNED UP WITH A TEMP AGENCY AND STARTED TAKING REAL ESTATE CLASSES ONLINE. I EVEN JOINED A GYM, WHICH IS WHERE I MET RON.
DAMN IT. WHY WON'T THIS RESET?
BEEP BEEP BEEP
HE WAS EXACTLY WHAT I WAS LOOKING FOR: ENTHUSIASTIC, POSITIVE--THE KIND OF GUY WHO COULD HAVE FUN ANYWHERE. HE WAS LIKE A BIG KID EXCEPT THAT HE HAD A REALLY COOL CAREER THAT HE WAS AMBITIOUS AND PASSIONATE ABOUT.
JUICE B
I'M FREELANCE, BUT I MAINLY WORK FOR DISNEY.
THE SCRIPT I'M WRITING NOW IS EXTRA BRUTAL 'CAUSE IT'S A PREQUEL, BUT ALSO KIND OF A REBOOT.
I TRIED TELLING THE SUITS **MY** THEORY, WHICH IS THAT ALL REBOOTS ARE STILL SEQUELS, IN A WAY...AND THEIR FRICKIN' HEADS BASICALLY EXPLODED! HA HA
EVENTUALLY I FOUND OUT THAT HE WAS WRITING COMPLETELY "ON SPEC." (AND THAT HIS REAL JOB WAS SELLING CHURROS AT DISNEYLAND), BUT BY THEN I'D ALREADY GOTTEN TOO ATTACHED TO CARE.

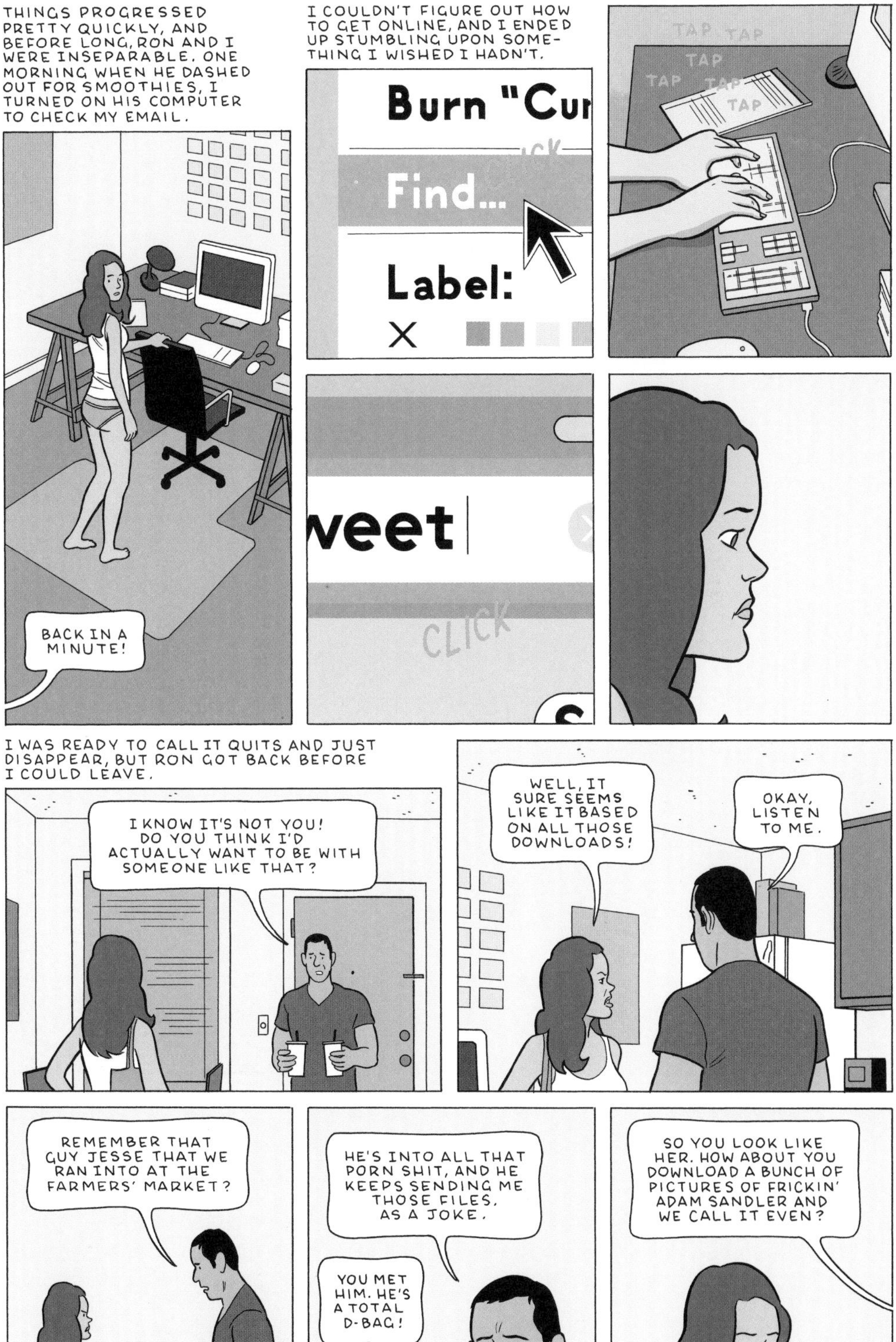
THINGS PROGRESSED PRETTY QUICKLY, AND BEFORE LONG, RON AND I WERE INSEPARABLE. ONE MORNING WHEN HE DASHED OUT FOR SMOOTHIES, I TURNED ON HIS COMPUTER TO CHECK MY EMAIL.
BACK IN A MINUTE!
I COULDN'T FIGURE OUT HOW TO GET ONLINE, AND I ENDED UP STUMBLING UPON SOMETHING I WISHED I HADN'T.
Burn "Cu
Find...
Label:
X
TAP TAP TAP TAP TAP TAP
weet
CLICK
I WAS READY TO CALL IT QUITS AND JUST DISAPPEAR, BUT RON GOT BACK BEFORE I COULD LEAVE.
I KNOW IT'S NOT YOU! DO YOU THINK I'D ACTUALLY WANT TO BE WITH SOMEONE LIKE THAT?
WELL, IT SURE SEEMS LIKE IT BASED ON ALL THOSE DOWNLOADS!
OKAY, LISTEN TO ME.
REMEMBER THAT GUY JESSE THAT WE RAN INTO AT THE FARMERS' MARKET?
HE'S INTO ALL THAT PORN SHIT, AND HE KEEPS SENDING ME THOSE FILES, AS A JOKE.
YOU MET HIM. HE'S A TOTAL D-BAG!
SO YOU LOOK LIKE HER. HOW ABOUT YOU DOWNLOAD A BUNCH OF PICTURES OF FRICKIN' ADAM SANDLER AND WE CALL IT EVEN?

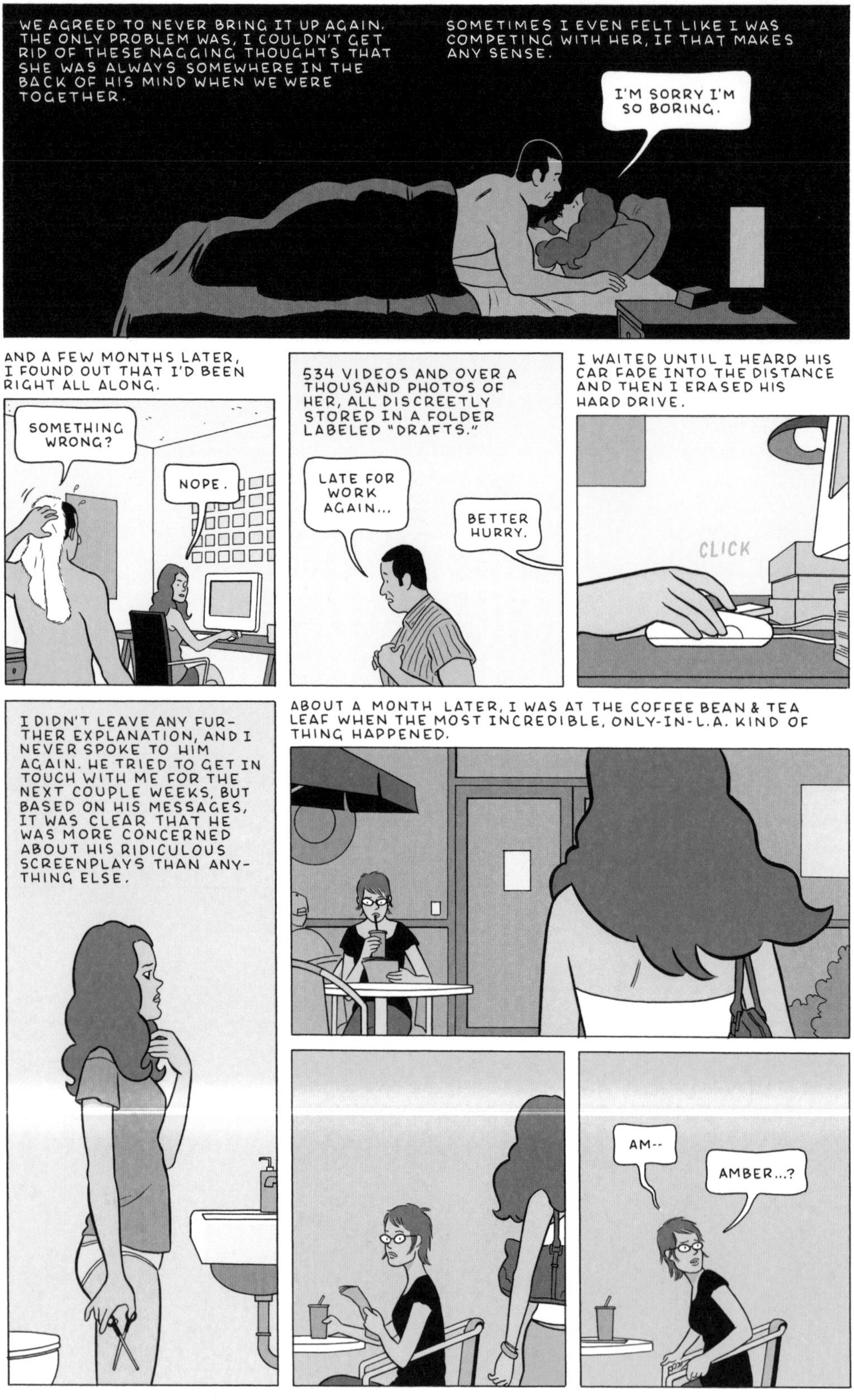
WE AGREED TO NEVER BRING IT UP AGAIN. THE ONLY PROBLEM WAS, I COULDN'T GET RID OF THESE NAGGING THOUGHTS THAT SHE WAS ALWAYS SOMEWHERE IN THE BACK OF HIS MIND WHEN WE WERE TOGETHER.
SOMETIMES I EVEN FELT LIKE I WAS COMPETING WITH HER, IF THAT MAKES ANY SENSE.
I'M SORRY I'M SO BORING.
AND A FEW MONTHS LATER, I FOUND OUT THAT I'D BEEN RIGHT ALL ALONG.
SOMETHING WRONG?
NOPE.
534 VIDEOS AND OVER A THOUSAND PHOTOS OF HER, ALL DISCREETLY STORED IN A FOLDER LABELED "DRAFTS."
LATE FOR WORK AGAIN...
BETTER HURRY.
I WAITED UNTIL I HEARD HIS CAR FADE INTO THE DISTANCE AND THEN I ERASED HIS HARD DRIVE.
CLICK
I DIDN'T LEAVE ANY FURTHER EXPLANATION, AND I NEVER SPOKE TO HIM AGAIN. HE TRIED TO GET IN TOUCH WITH ME FOR THE NEXT COUPLE WEEKS, BUT BASED ON HIS MESSAGES, IT WAS CLEAR THAT HE WAS MORE CONCERNED ABOUT HIS RIDICULOUS SCREENPLAYS THAN ANYTHING ELSE.
ABOUT A MONTH LATER, I WAS AT THE COFFEE BEAN & TEA LEAF WHEN THE MOST INCREDIBLE, ONLY-IN-L.A. KIND OF THING HAPPENED.
AM--
AMBER...?

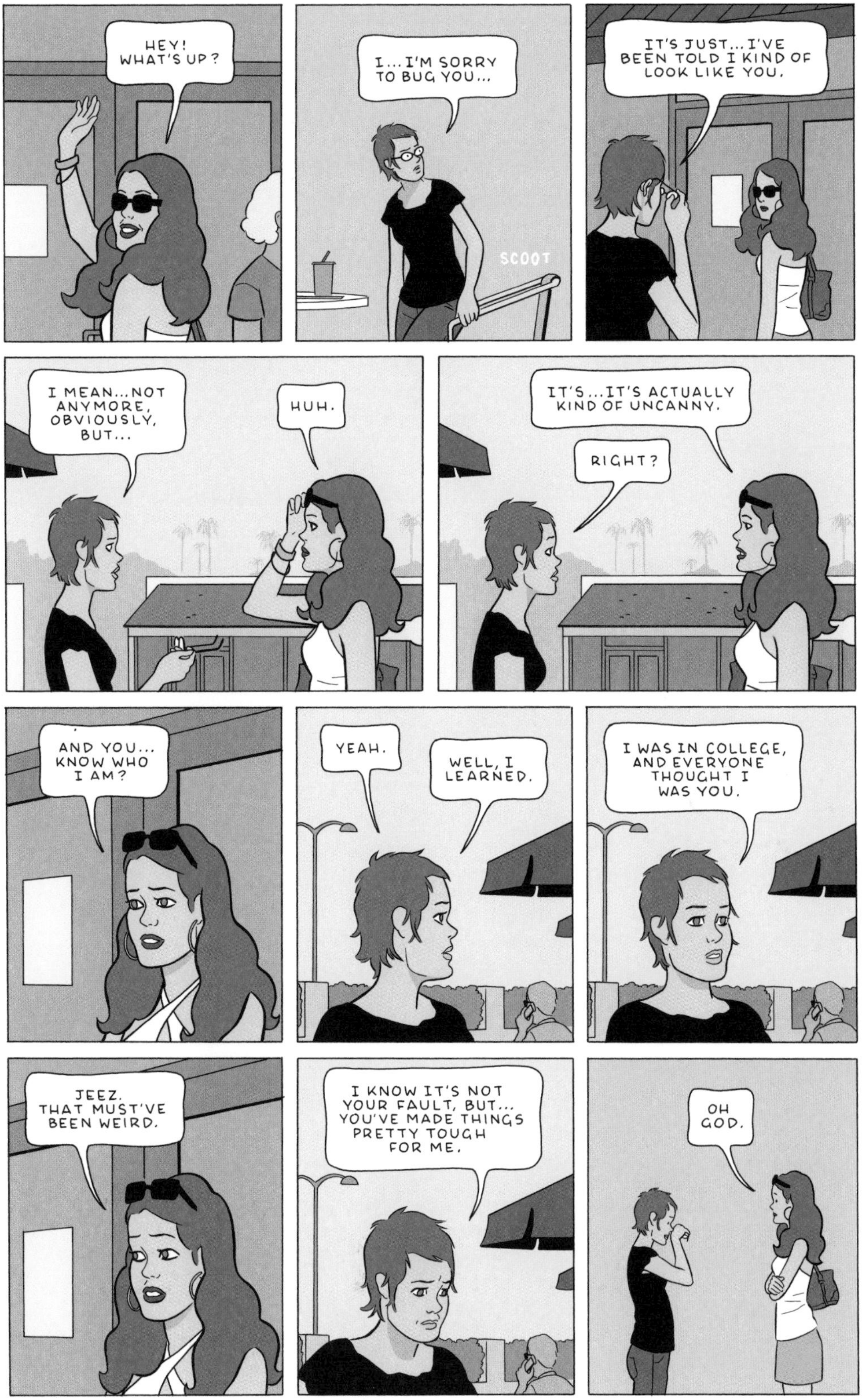
HEY! WHAT'S UP?
I... I'M SORRY TO BUG YOU...
SCOOT
IT'S JUST... I'VE BEEN TOLD I KIND OF LOOK LIKE YOU.
I MEAN... NOT ANYMORE, OBVIOUSLY, BUT...
HUH.
IT'S... IT'S ACTUALLY KIND OF UNCANNY.
RIGHT?
AND YOU... KNOW WHO I AM?
YEAH.
WELL, I LEARNED.
I WAS IN COLLEGE, AND EVERYONE THOUGHT I WAS YOU.
JEEZ. THAT MUST'VE BEEN WEIRD.
I KNOW IT'S NOT YOUR FAULT, BUT... YOU'VE MADE THINGS PRETTY TOUGH FOR ME.
OH GOD.

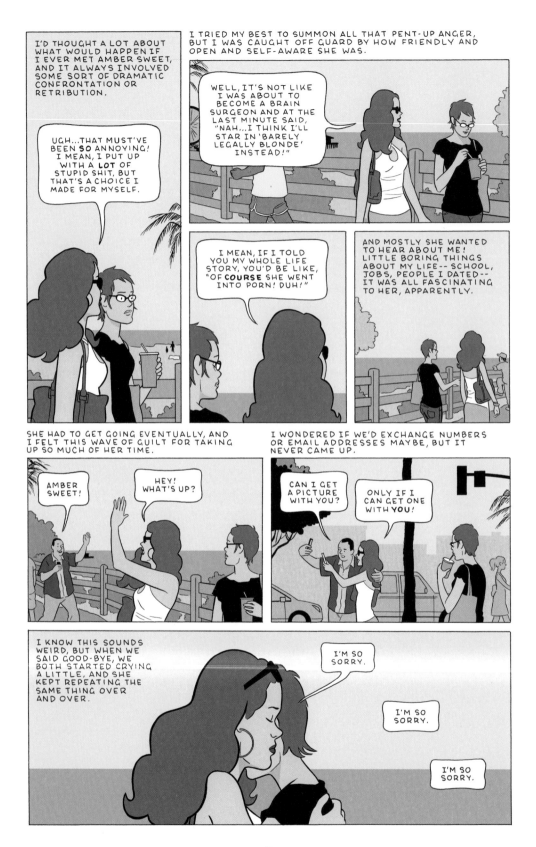

I'D THOUGHT A LOT ABOUT WHAT WOULD HAPPEN IF I EVER MET AMBER SWEET, AND IT ALWAYS INVOLVED SOME SORT OF DRAMATIC CONFRONTATION OR RETRIBUTION.

I TRIED MY BEST TO SUMMON ALL THAT PENT-UP ANGER, BUT I WAS CAUGHT OFF GUARD BY HOW FRIENDLY AND OPEN AND SELF-AWARE SHE WAS.

WELL, IT'S NOT LIKE I WAS ABOUT TO BECOME A BRAIN SURGEON AND AT THE LAST MINUTE SAID, "NAH...I THINK I'LL STAR IN 'BARELY LEGALLY BLONDE' INSTEAD!"

UGH...THAT MUST'VE BEEN **SO** ANNOYING! I MEAN, I PUT UP WITH A **LOT** OF STUPID SHIT, BUT THAT'S A CHOICE I MADE FOR MYSELF.

I MEAN, IF I TOLD YOU MY WHOLE LIFE STORY, YOU'D BE LIKE, "OF **COURSE** SHE WENT INTO PORN! DUH!"

AND MOSTLY SHE WANTED TO HEAR ABOUT ME! LITTLE BORING THINGS ABOUT MY LIFE-- SCHOOL, JOBS, PEOPLE I DATED-- IT WAS ALL FASCINATING TO HER, APPARENTLY.

SHE HAD TO GET GOING EVENTUALLY, AND I FELT THIS WAVE OF GUILT FOR TAKING UP SO MUCH OF HER TIME.

AMBER SWEET!

HEY! WHAT'S UP?

I WONDERED IF WE'D EXCHANGE NUMBERS OR EMAIL ADDRESSES MAYBE, BUT IT NEVER CAME UP.

CAN I GET A PICTURE WITH YOU?

ONLY IF I CAN GET ONE WITH **YOU!**

I KNOW THIS SOUNDS WEIRD, BUT WHEN WE SAID GOOD-BYE, WE BOTH STARTED CRYING A LITTLE, AND SHE KEPT REPEATING THE SAME THING OVER AND OVER.

I'M SO SORRY.

I'M SO SORRY.

I'M SO SORRY.

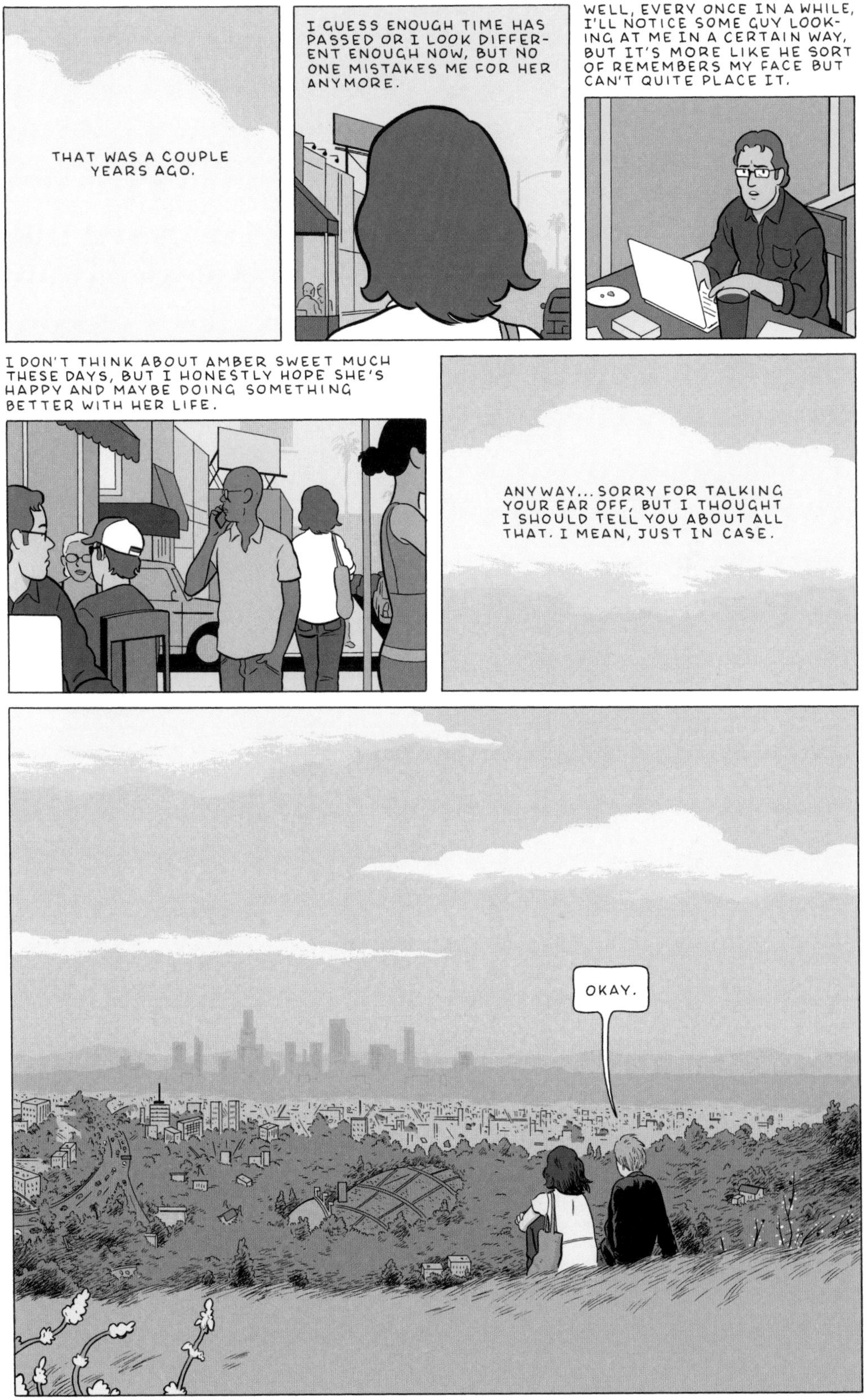
THAT WAS A COUPLE YEARS AGO.
I GUESS ENOUGH TIME HAS PASSED OR I LOOK DIFFERENT ENOUGH NOW, BUT NO ONE MISTAKES ME FOR HER ANYMORE.
WELL, EVERY ONCE IN A WHILE, I'LL NOTICE SOME GUY LOOKING AT ME IN A CERTAIN WAY, BUT IT'S MORE LIKE HE SORT OF REMEMBERS MY FACE BUT CAN'T QUITE PLACE IT.
I DON'T THINK ABOUT AMBER SWEET MUCH THESE DAYS, BUT I HONESTLY HOPE SHE'S HAPPY AND MAYBE DOING SOMETHING BETTER WITH HER LIFE.
ANYWAY... SORRY FOR TALKING YOUR EAR OFF, BUT I THOUGHT I SHOULD TELL YOU ABOUT ALL THAT. I MEAN, JUST IN CASE.
OKAY.

GO OWLS

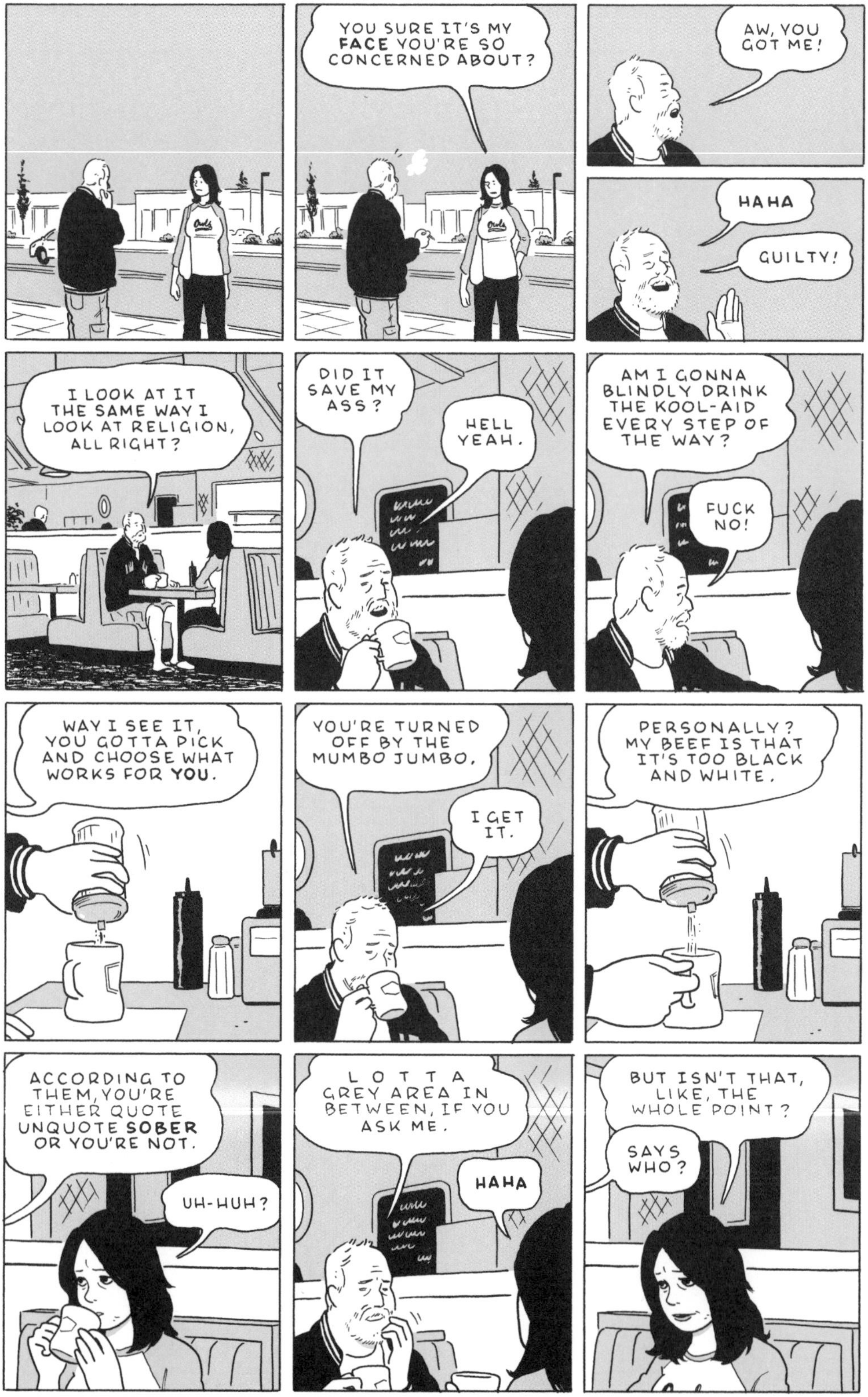
YOU SURE IT'S MY FACE YOU'RE SO CONCERNED ABOUT?
AW, YOU GOT ME!
HAHA
GUILTY!
I LOOK AT IT THE SAME WAY I LOOK AT RELIGION, ALL RIGHT?
DID IT SAVE MY ASS?
HELL YEAH.
AM I GONNA BLINDLY DRINK THE KOOL-AID EVERY STEP OF THE WAY?
FUCK NO!
WAY I SEE IT, YOU GOTTA PICK AND CHOOSE WHAT WORKS FOR YOU.
YOU'RE TURNED OFF BY THE MUMBO JUMBO.
I GET IT.
PERSONALLY? MY BEEF IS THAT IT'S TOO BLACK AND WHITE.
ACCORDING TO THEM, YOU'RE EITHER QUOTE UNQUOTE SOBER OR YOU'RE NOT.
UH-HUH?
L O T T A GREY AREA IN BETWEEN, IF YOU ASK ME.
HAHA
BUT ISN'T THAT, LIKE, THE WHOLE POINT?
SAYS WHO?

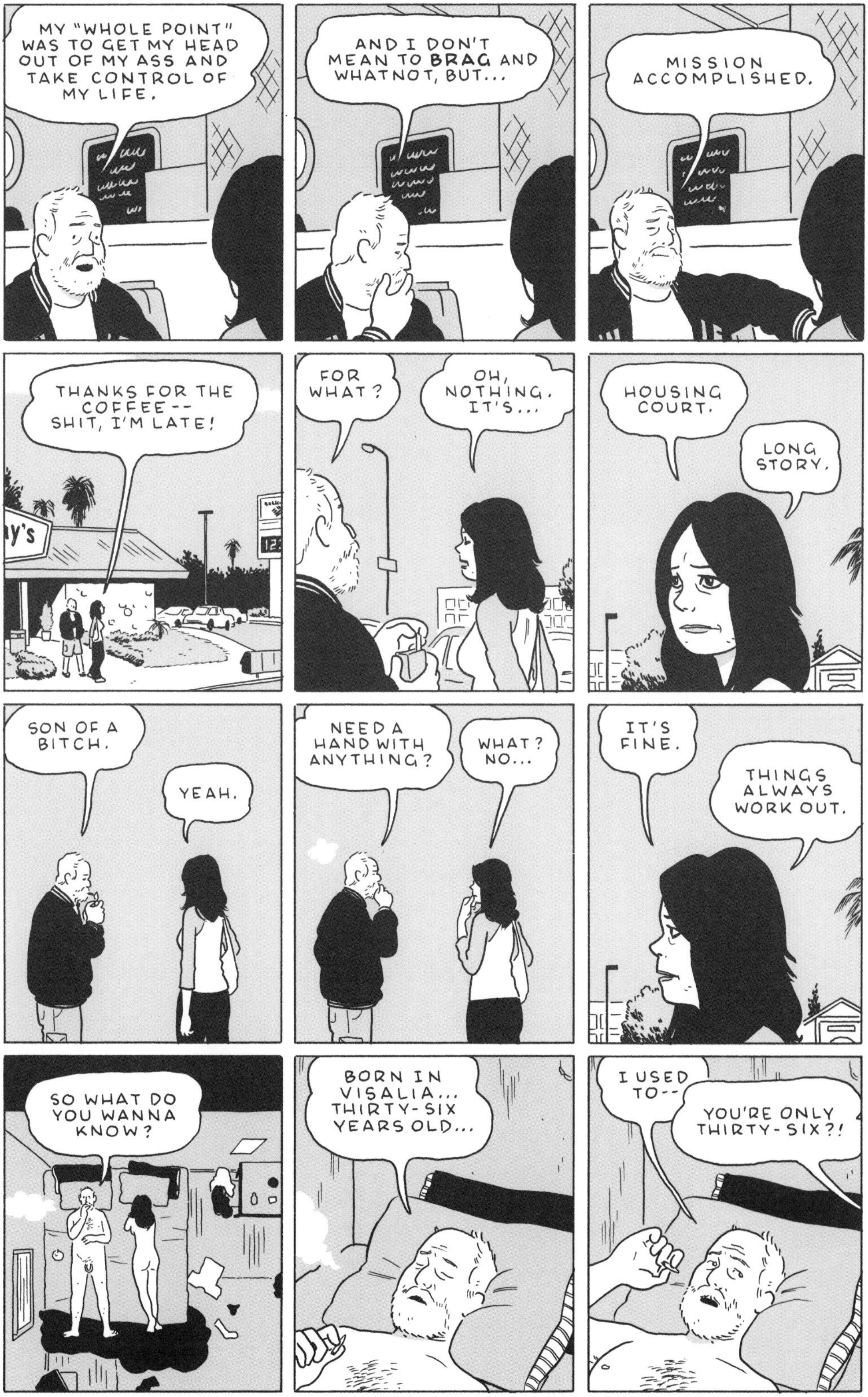
MY "WHOLE POINT" WAS TO GET MY HEAD OUT OF MY ASS AND TAKE CONTROL OF MY LIFE.
AND I DON'T MEAN TO **BRAG** AND WHATNOT, BUT...
MISSION ACCOMPLISHED.
THANKS FOR THE COFFEE-- SHIT, I'M LATE!
FOR WHAT?
OH, NOTHING. IT'S...
HOUSING COURT.
LONG STORY.
SON OF A BITCH.
YEAH.
NEED A HAND WITH ANYTHING?
WHAT? NO...
IT'S FINE.
THINGS ALWAYS WORK OUT.
SO WHAT DO YOU WANNA KNOW?
BORN IN VISALIA... THIRTY-SIX YEARS OLD...
I USED TO--
YOU'RE ONLY THIRTY-SIX?!

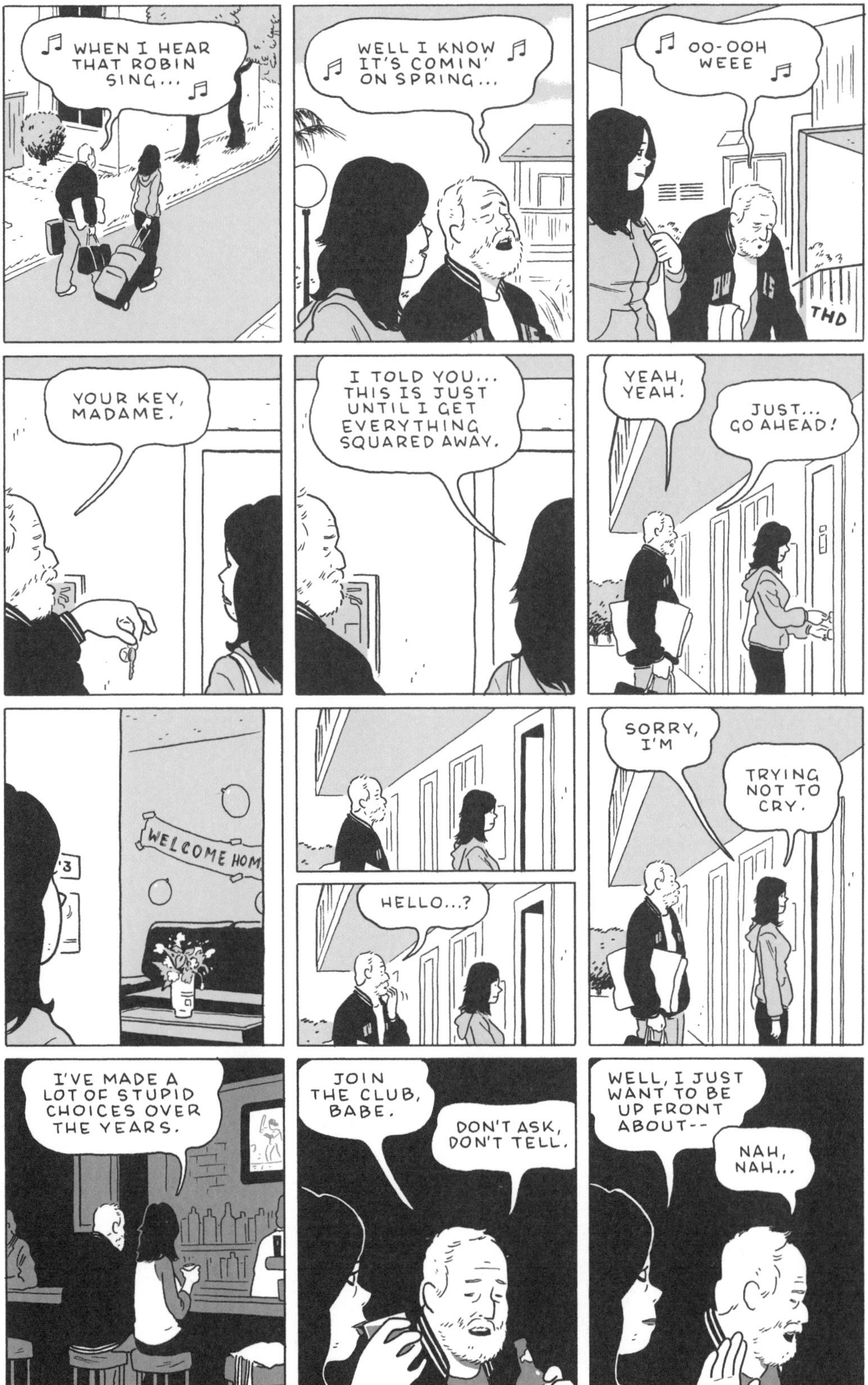
♫ WHEN I HEAR THAT ROBIN SING... ♫
WELL I KNOW IT'S COMIN' ON SPRING... ♫ ♫
♫ OO-OOH WEEE ♫
THD
YOUR KEY, MADAME.
I TOLD YOU... THIS IS JUST UNTIL I GET EVERYTHING SQUARED AWAY.
YEAH, YEAH.
JUST... GO AHEAD!
WELCOME HOM
HELLO...?
SORRY, I'M
TRYING NOT TO CRY.
I'VE MADE A LOT OF STUPID CHOICES OVER THE YEARS.
JOIN THE CLUB, BABE.
DON'T ASK, DON'T TELL.
WELL, I JUST WANT TO BE UP FRONT ABOUT--
NAH, NAH...

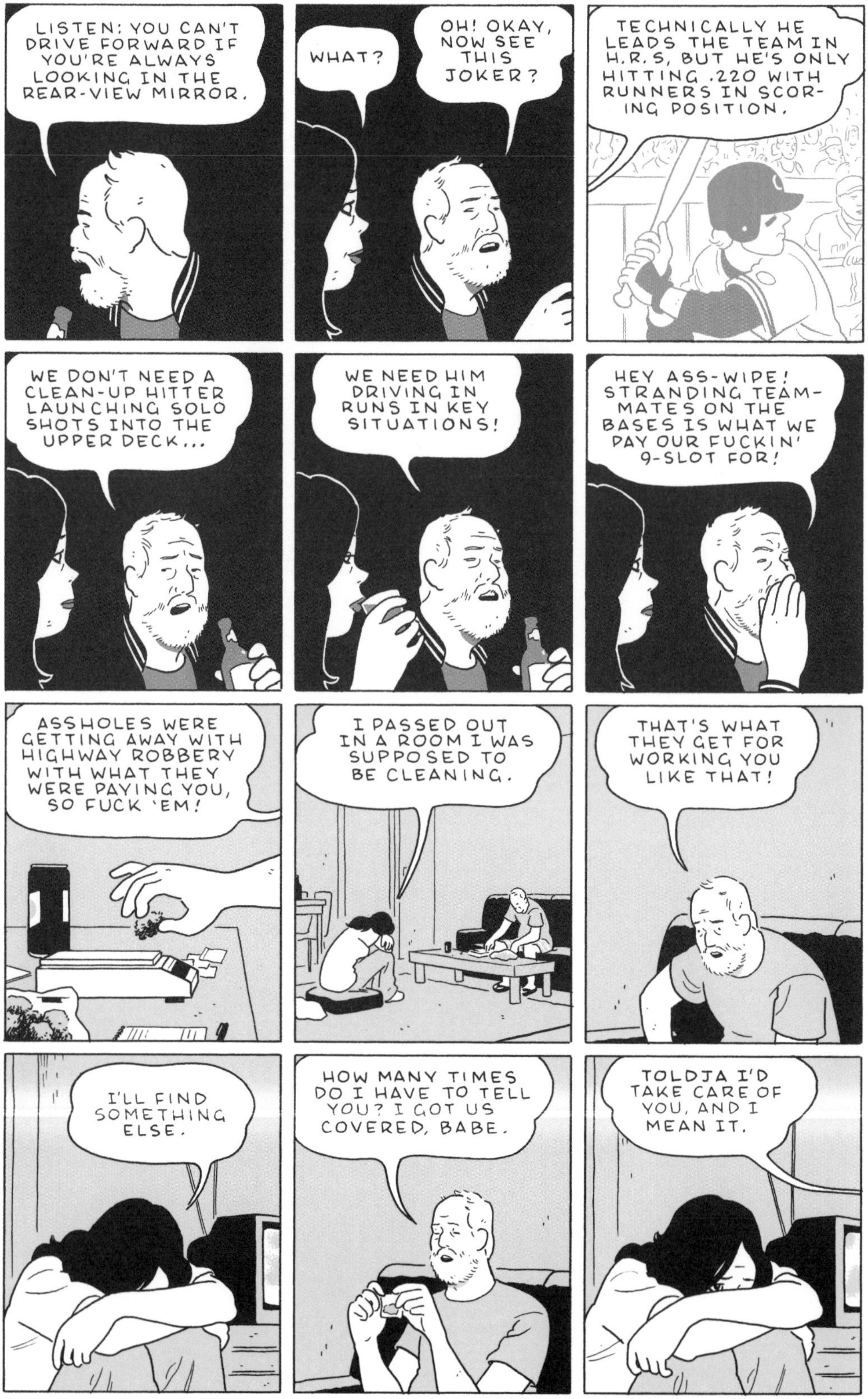
LISTEN: YOU CAN'T DRIVE FORWARD IF YOU'RE ALWAYS LOOKING IN THE REAR-VIEW MIRROR.
WHAT?
OH! OKAY, NOW SEE THIS JOKER?
TECHNICALLY HE LEADS THE TEAM IN H.R.S, BUT HE'S ONLY HITTING .220 WITH RUNNERS IN SCORING POSITION.
WE DON'T NEED A CLEAN-UP HITTER LAUNCHING SOLO SHOTS INTO THE UPPER DECK...
WE NEED HIM DRIVING IN RUNS IN KEY SITUATIONS!
HEY ASS-WIPE! STRANDING TEAM-MATES ON THE BASES IS WHAT WE PAY OUR FUCKIN' 9-SLOT FOR!
ASSHOLES WERE GETTING AWAY WITH HIGHWAY ROBBERY WITH WHAT THEY WERE PAYING YOU, SO FUCK 'EM!
I PASSED OUT IN A ROOM I WAS SUPPOSED TO BE CLEANING.
THAT'S WHAT THEY GET FOR WORKING YOU LIKE THAT!
I'LL FIND SOMETHING ELSE.
HOW MANY TIMES DO I HAVE TO TELL YOU? I GOT US COVERED, BABE.
TOLDJA I'D TAKE CARE OF YOU, AND I MEAN IT.

59

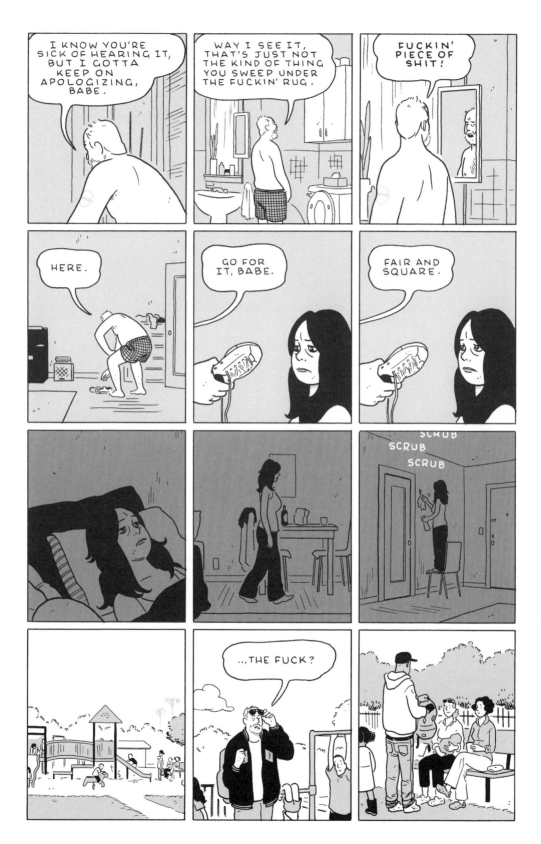

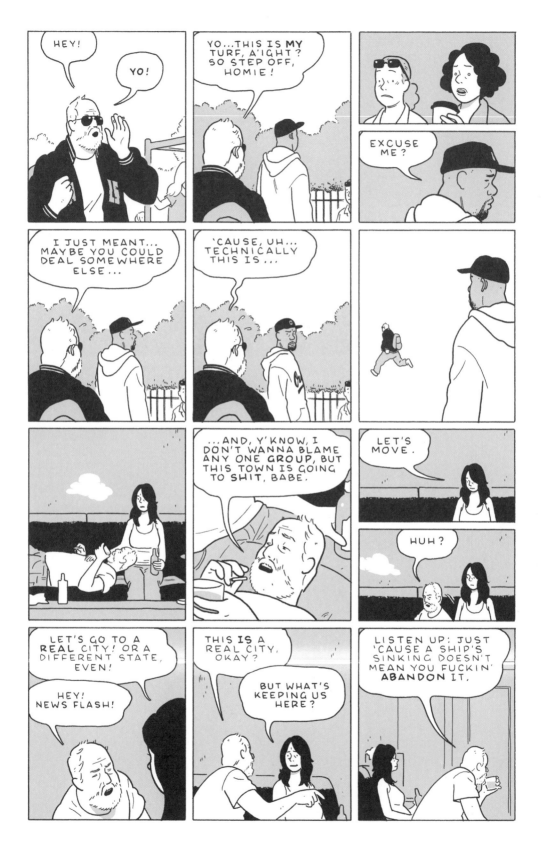

二月に気持ちの整理がついて全てを良く
考えられる様になった時には、カリフォルニア
に帰る事に決めました。あなたのお婆さん
と伯母さんと伯父さん達は皆この選択
には反対で、お互いに気まずいまま別れ
ました。でもそれは仕方のない事でした。

TRANSLATED,

from the JAPANESE,

IN FEBRUARY, WHEN MY MIND WAS UNCLOUDED ENOUGH TO APPRAISE EVERYTHING, I DECIDED WE WOULD RETURN TO CALIFORNIA. YOUR GRANDMOTHER, AUNT, AND UNCLE DID NOT AGREE WITH THIS CHOICE, AND WE LEFT ON UNHAPPY TERMS. IT WAS ALL VERY UNDERSTANDABLE.

ON OUR PREVIOUS FLIGHT, IN THE OPPOSITE DIRECTION, YOU SLEPT AND SQUIRMED ON TOP OF MY LEGS. WHAT A SURPRISE WHEN THE AIRLINE TOLD ME YOU WERE TOO OLD FOR THAT NOW, AND I WAS REQUIRED TO PURCHASE A SEAT FOR YOU. IT WAS COSTLY, BUT I THINK A RELIEF TO BOTH OF US.

I WORRIED ABOUT SITTING NEXT TO PEOPLE WHO DID NOT LIKE CHILDREN, BUT THE MAN IN OUR ROW WAS CHEERFUL TOWARD YOU IMMEDIATELY. HE WAS A UNIVERSITY PROFESSOR, FROM OSAKA ORIGINALLY, ON HIS WAY TO A CONFERENCE IN BERKELEY. HE AND I EXCHANGED A FEW NICE WORDS, BUT HE WAS ESPECIALLY HAPPY INTERACTING WITH YOU.

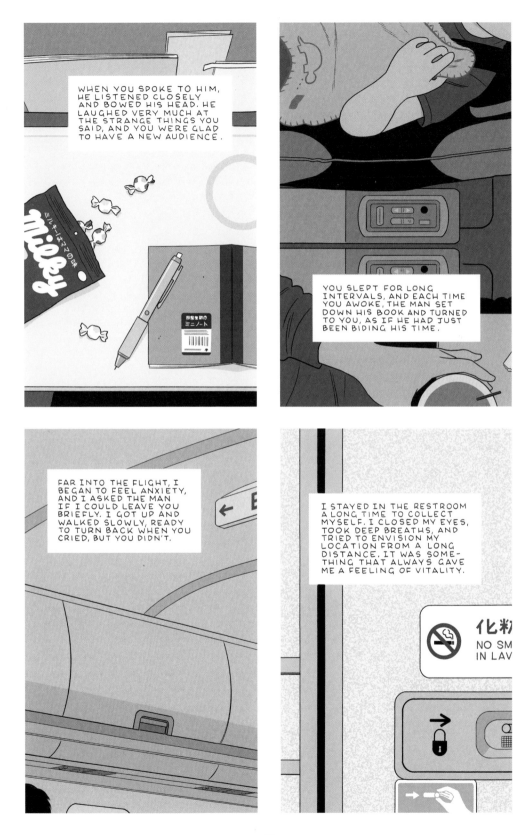

WHEN YOU SPOKE TO HIM, HE LISTENED CLOSELY AND BOWED HIS HEAD. HE LAUGHED VERY MUCH AT THE STRANGE THINGS YOU SAID, AND YOU WERE GLAD TO HAVE A NEW AUDIENCE.

YOU SLEPT FOR LONG INTERVALS, AND EACH TIME YOU AWOKE, THE MAN SET DOWN HIS BOOK AND TURNED TO YOU, AS IF HE HAD JUST BEEN BIDING HIS TIME.

FAR INTO THE FLIGHT, I BEGAN TO FEEL ANXIETY, AND I ASKED THE MAN IF I COULD LEAVE YOU BRIEFLY. I GOT UP AND WALKED SLOWLY, READY TO TURN BACK WHEN YOU CRIED, BUT YOU DIDN'T.

I STAYED IN THE RESTROOM A LONG TIME TO COLLECT MYSELF. I CLOSED MY EYES, TOOK DEEP BREATHS, AND TRIED TO ENVISION MY LOCATION FROM A LONG DISTANCE. IT WAS SOME-THING THAT ALWAYS GAVE ME A FEELING OF VITALITY.

NO SM
IN LAV

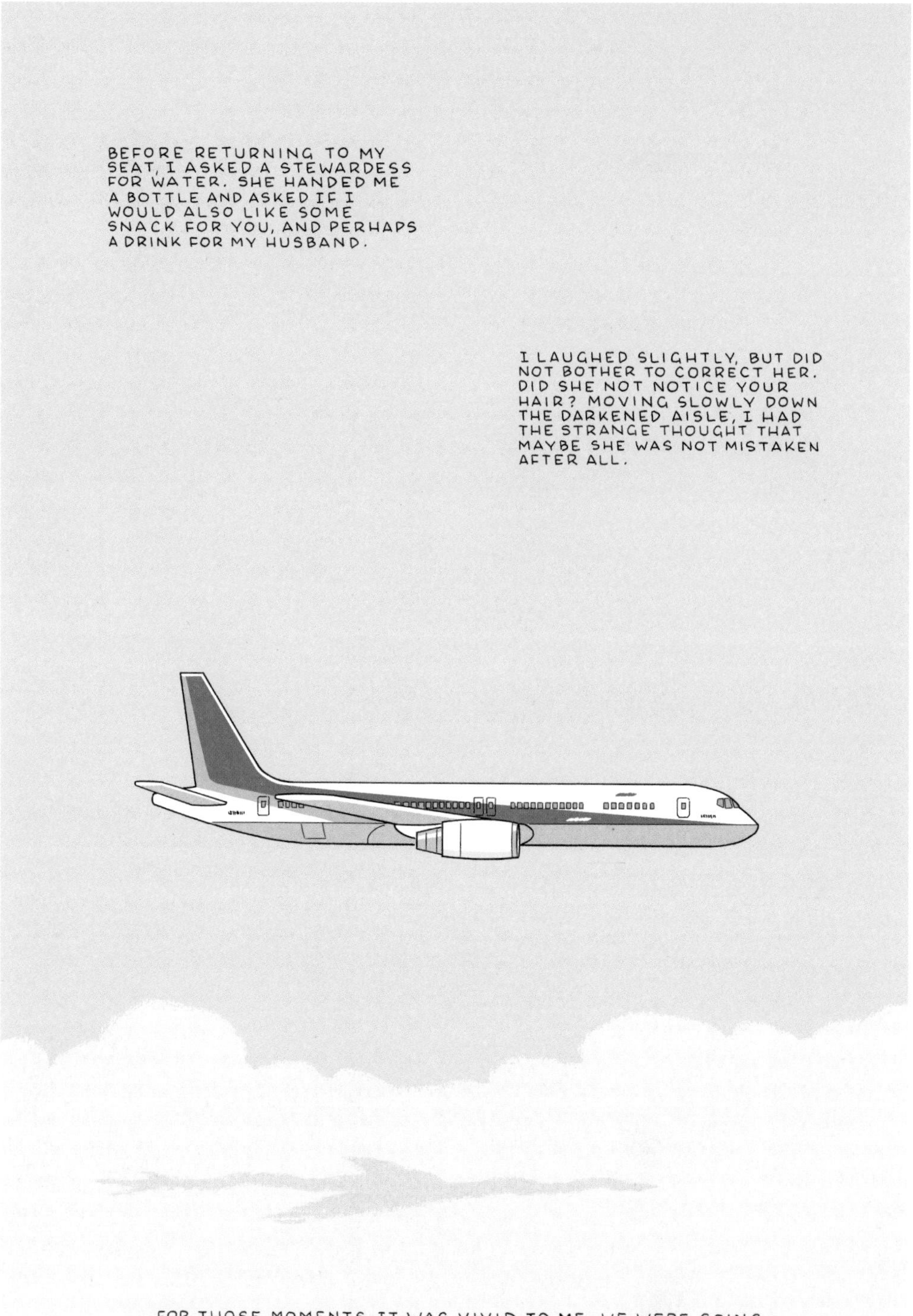

BEFORE RETURNING TO MY
SEAT, I ASKED A STEWARDESS
FOR WATER. SHE HANDED ME
A BOTTLE AND ASKED IF I
WOULD ALSO LIKE SOME
SNACK FOR YOU, AND PERHAPS
A DRINK FOR MY HUSBAND.

I LAUGHED SLIGHTLY, BUT DID
NOT BOTHER TO CORRECT HER.
DID SHE NOT NOTICE YOUR
HAIR? MOVING SLOWLY DOWN
THE DARKENED AISLE, I HAD
THE STRANGE THOUGHT THAT
MAYBE SHE WAS NOT MISTAKEN
AFTER ALL.

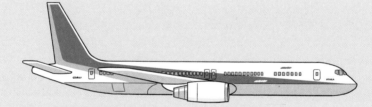

FOR THOSE MOMENTS, IT WAS VIVID TO ME. WE WERE GOING
ON VACATION TO AMERICA: ME, YOU, AND YOUR FATHER, A
UNIVERSITY PROFESSOR FROM OSAKA.

WHEN WE LANDED, THE PROFESSOR LEFT THE PLANE WITH US IN SILENCE. AFTER TWELVE HOURS TOGETHER, HE WAS A STRANGER AGAIN. HE BOWED TO US BOTH AND DISAPPEARED INTO THE CROWD OF PEOPLE WAITING FOR TAXI CABS.

YOUR FATHER WAS WAITING AT THE BAGGAGE CLAIM AREA, AS HE SAID HE WOULD BE. HE LOOKED LIKE HE HAD JUST WOKEN UP. YOU ASKED ME FOR PERMISSION BEFORE RUNNING TO HIM.

I HAD NOT THOUGHT AHEAD TO THAT MOMENT SOMEHOW. STANDING THERE ALONE, I WANTED TO BE INVISIBLE, TO EVAPORATE.

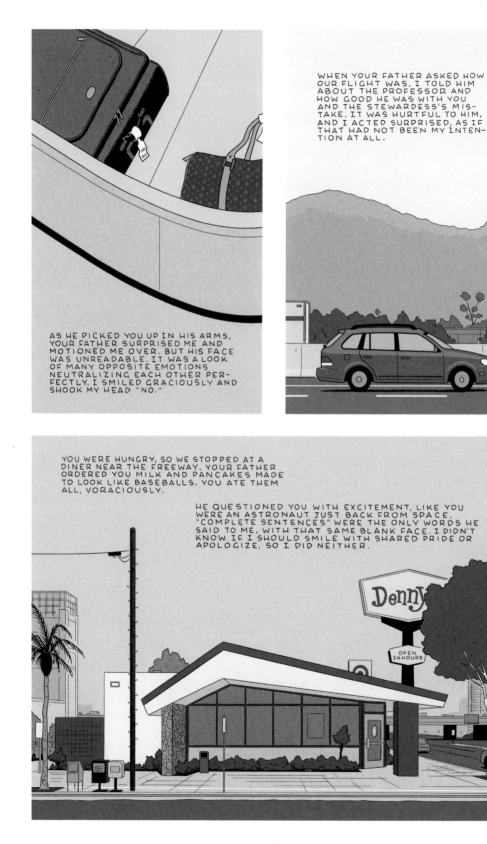

WHEN YOUR FATHER ASKED HOW OUR FLIGHT WAS, I TOLD HIM ABOUT THE PROFESSOR AND HOW GOOD HE WAS WITH YOU AND THE STEWARDESS'S MISTAKE. IT WAS HURTFUL TO HIM, AND I ACTED SURPRISED, AS IF THAT HAD NOT BEEN MY INTENTION AT ALL.

AS HE PICKED YOU UP IN HIS ARMS, YOUR FATHER SURPRISED ME AND MOTIONED ME OVER. BUT HIS FACE WAS UNREADABLE. IT WAS A LOOK OF MANY OPPOSITE EMOTIONS NEUTRALIZING EACH OTHER PERFECTLY. I SMILED GRACIOUSLY AND SHOOK MY HEAD "NO."

YOU WERE HUNGRY, SO WE STOPPED AT A DINER NEAR THE FREEWAY. YOUR FATHER ORDERED YOU MILK AND PANCAKES MADE TO LOOK LIKE BASEBALLS. YOU ATE THEM ALL, VORACIOUSLY.

HE QUESTIONED YOU WITH EXCITEMENT, LIKE YOU WERE AN ASTRONAUT JUST BACK FROM SPACE. "COMPLETE SENTENCES" WERE THE ONLY WORDS HE SAID TO ME, WITH THAT SAME BLANK FACE. I DIDN'T KNOW IF I SHOULD SMILE WITH SHARED PRIDE OR APOLOGIZE, SO I DID NEITHER.

THEN YOUR FATHER DROVE US TO THE TINY APARTMENT HE
HAD FOUND FOR US. HE KEPT THE CAR MOTOR ON AND
CARRIED OUR LUGGAGE INSIDE QUICKLY. IN THE
MORNING, HE WOULD PICK YOU UP AND TAKE YOU TO OUR
OLD HOME FOR AN EXTRAVAGANT BELATED BIRTHDAY
PARTY WITH THE NEIGHBORHOOD CHILDREN AND YOUR
CALIFORNIA GRANDPARENTS.

I WAS UPSET BY OUR SHABBY, UNFAMILIAR
SURROUNDINGS. YOUR CHEERFUL INDIFFER-
ENCE TO IT ALL MADE ME CRUMPLE. I HAD
ENOUGH STRENGTH TO GIVE YOU A BATH AND
PUT YOU TO BED, AND THEN I FELL ASLEEP IN
MY CLOTHES ON THE FLOOR BESIDE YOU,
LISTENING TO THE SOUND OF YOUR BREATH.

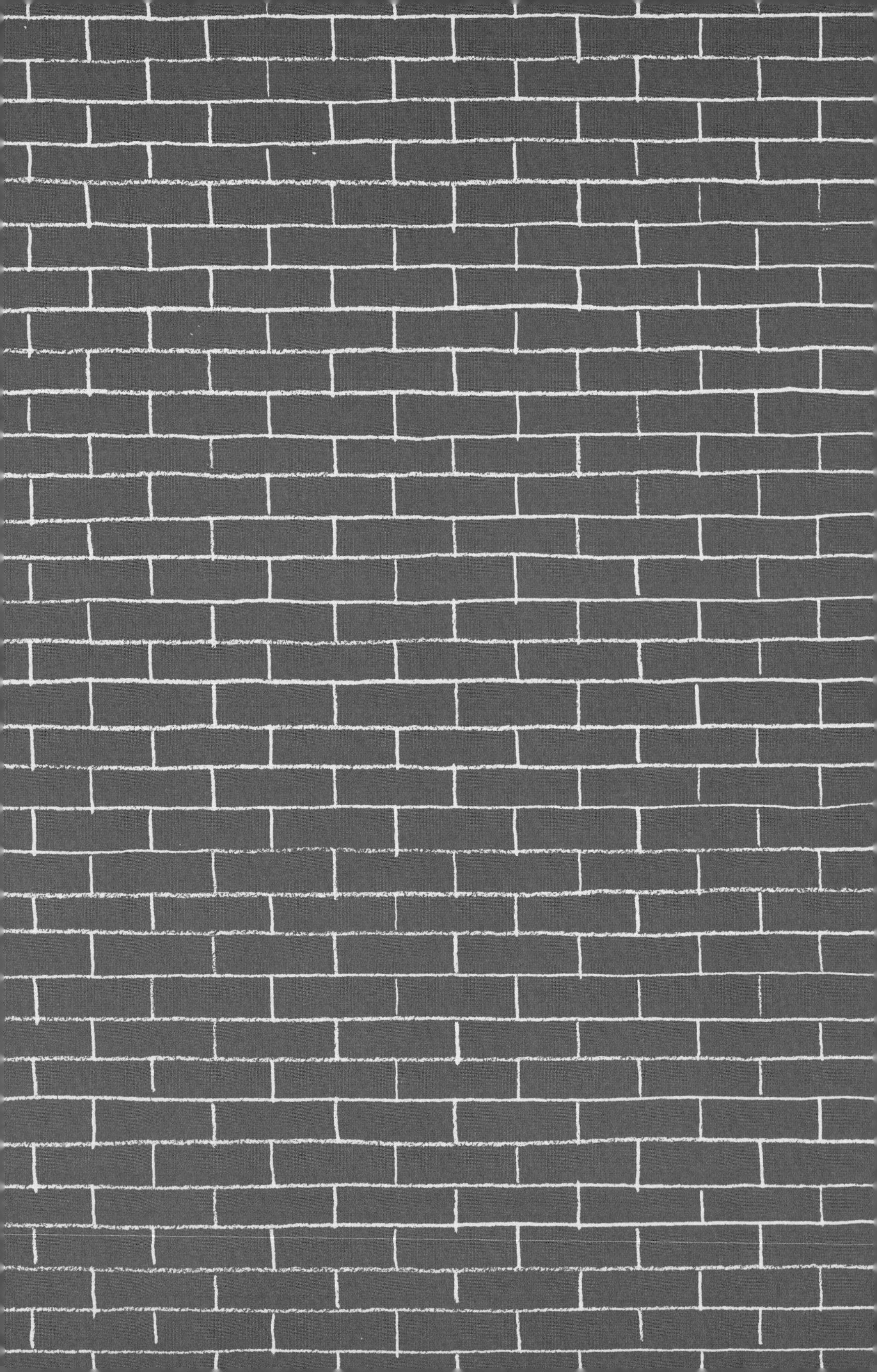

KILLING and DYING

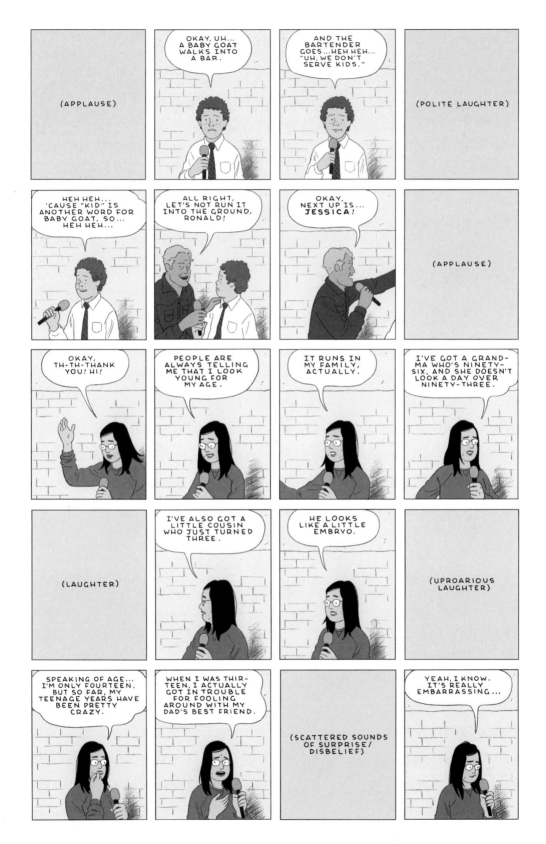

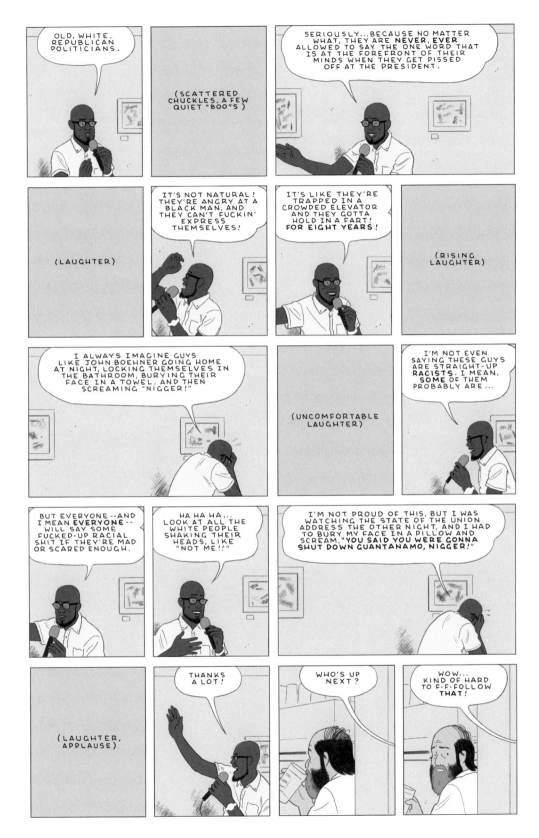

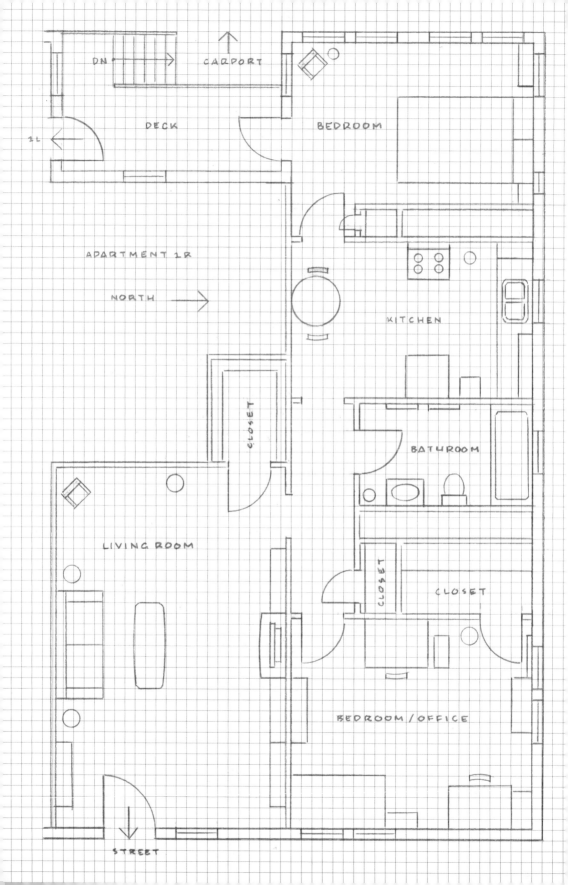

DN → CARPORT ↑

DECK

1L ←

BEDROOM

APARTMENT 1R

NORTH →

KITCHEN

CLOSET

BATHROOM

LIVING ROOM

CLOSET

CLOSET

BEDROOM/OFFICE

↓
STREET

INTRUDERS

*for Yoshihiro Tatsumi*

BETWEEN MY SECOND AND THIRD TOURS, I CAME BACK TO A BUNCH OF BULLSHIT AND NOT MUCH ELSE.

I HAD A COUSIN WHO LET ME CRASH IN HER BASEMENT. SHE WAS MARRIED WITH THREE KIDS.

ONE NIGHT I HEARD THEM ALL TALKING ABOUT ME THROUGH THE CEILING, AND SOME OF THE THINGS THEY SAID JUST ABOUT KILLED ME.

I ENDED UP AT A PLACE CALLED EXTENDED STAY AMERICA, OUT BY THE CAR DEALERSHIPS AND STRIP MALLS.

RIGHT ACROSS THE FREEWAY WAS AN IN-N-OUT, A KRISPY KREME, AND A PANDA EXPRESS.

I FIGURED WORSE CAME TO WORSE, I COULD ALWAYS EAT MYSELF TO DEATH AND THE AUTOPSY WOULD STILL COME BACK CLEAN.

ONE OF THOSE PLACES, THAT'S WHERE I RAN INTO THE GIRL, WHAT-EVER HER NAME WAS.

OH MY GOD!

I BLUFFED MY WAY THROUGH ABOUT TEN MINUTES OF SMALL TALK BEFORE IT FINALLY CLICKED.

I WAS TOTALLY JUST THINKING ABOUT YOU GUYS!

SHE WAS SOMEONE'S KID OR NIECE OR SOME-THING. SHE HOUSE-SAT FOR ME AND MARIA THAT TIME WE WENT TO CATALINA.

I WAS CLEANING OUT MY CAR, AND GUESS WHAT I FOUND!

I DIDN'T LIKE THE IDEA OF SOMEONE STAYING THERE, BUT MARIA HAD A THING ABOUT LEAVING THE APARTMENT EMPTY.

COME ON! I'M RIGHT OUTSIDE!

I WAS SUPPOSED TO GO PICK UP THE KEYS FROM THE GIRL WHEN WE GOT BACK, BUT I KEPT PUTTING IT OFF.

SO HOW IS MARIA?

GREAT! YEAH...

THEN SHE OFFERED TO DROP THEM BY SOMETIME, AND THEN MARIA WAS GONNA GET THEM, BUT EVENTUAL-LY WE ALL JUST FORGOT ABOUT IT.

I JUST THINK THIS IS SO CRAZY, RUNNING INTO YOU HERE!

THEY WERE JUST COPIES, ANYWAY, MADE AT THE HARD-WARE STORE FOR A BUCK A PIECE.

AMA-A-A-A-ZING!

TNK TNK

STANDING THERE IN THE PARKING LOT, I SHOULD'VE JUST BACKTRACKED AND EXPLAINED EVERY-THING, BUT THE RIGHT MOMENT NEVER CAME.

HA HA... FUCKIN' UNBELIEVABLE!

IN-C

I GUESS I GOT SWEPT UP IN HER EXCITE-MENT AND DIDN'T WANT TO MAKE THINGS AWKWARD.

OH!

I'M ACTUALLY SUPPOSED TO BE MEETING UP WITH MY BOYFRIEND, SO...

YEAH, I WASN'T--

NO, I JUST MEANT--

YOU DIDN'T HAVE TO SAY THAT.

BACK AT THE HOTEL, I STARED AT THE KEYS FOR AWHILE, THREW THEM IN THE TRASH, AND WENT TO SLEEP.

NEXT MORNING, I WOKE UP, DUG THE KEYS OUT OF THE TRASH, AND CAUGHT A BUS INTO TOWN.

THE CAFE ACROSS FROM OUR APARTMENT DIDN'T SELL COFFEE ANYMORE, THANKS TO THE NEW PEET'S UP THE BLOCK.

NOW THEY SPECIALIZED IN CREPES, SMOOTHIES, AND SOME SHIT CALLED BUBBLE TEA.

I WAS DYING FOR A COFFEE, BUT THE TRUTH IS, I WAS JUST THERE FOR THE VIEW.

IT WAS DEPRESSING TO SEE EVERYONE TRAPPED ON THE SAME HAMSTER WHEEL. GO TO WORK, COME HOME, REPEAT.

I TRACKED THE GUY IN OUR OLD PLACE FOR A WEEK, AND THE ONLY THING THAT CHANGED WAS THE COLOR OF HIS SUIT.

NO ONE REALLY GIVES A SHIT ABOUT RENTERS, BUT A DECENT LANDLORD WILL RE-KEY THE LOCKS AS A BASIC SECURITY MEASURE WHEN A PLACE TURNS OVER.

THE OLD CHINESE GUY WOULD'VE DONE IT. EVERYTHING WENT DOWNHILL WHEN HE CROAKED AND HIS SCUMBAG KIDS TOOK OVER.

WE HAD TO MAIL OUR KEYS TO THE DAUGHTER TO GET OUR DEPOSIT BACK WHEN WE LEFT, BUT SO WHAT?

IT SMELLED DIFFER-ENT. THAT'S WHAT I NOTICED BEFORE ANYTHING ELSE.

ONCE I MADE SURE THE PLACE WAS EMPTY, I OPENED A FEW WINDOWS TO AIR IT OUT.

EVERYTHING WAS UP-GRADED, REPAIRED, RE-DONE. MARIA WOULD'VE LOVED IT.

THINGS THAT WE LEARNED TO LIVE WITH, LIKE THE PEELING PAINT IN THE BATHROOM AND THE BROKEN LIGHT IN THE FRIDGE, HAD ALL BEEN TAKEN CARE OF.

BUT THERE WAS ENOUGH THAT HADN'T CHANGED: SAME FIX-TURES, SAME APPLI-ANCES, SAME SHIT-BROWN CARPET IN THE BEDROOM.

I FOUND THE HOLE IN THE WALL THAT I'D PUNCHED AND THEN PUTTIED OVER. THE BATHROOM SHELF I PUT UP WAS STILL THERE.

THE GUY EVEN KEPT THE COBWEBBY PIECE OF 2X4 I USED TO PROP THE KITCHEN WINDOW OPEN.

I COULD'VE SNOOPED AROUND, TURNED ON THE COMPUTER, RIFLED THROUGH THE DRAWERS, BUT THAT'S A LINE I WOULDN'T CROSS.

THERE'S A MILLION THINGS I COULD'VE DONE, BUT I'D SATIS-FIED MY CURIOSITY AND THAT WAS THAT.

I COULDN'T SLEEP THAT NIGHT, AND THE SAME STUPID THOUGHT KEPT RATTLING AROUND IN MY HEAD: THAT THE GUY WOULD COME HOME AND NOTICE THE MISSING EGG.

OF COURSE THE PROBABILITY OF THAT WAS SLIM, AND PLUS, WHAT WAS HE GONNA DO? CALL THE COPS TO REPORT IT?

BUT I'D BEEN CARELESS AND IT NAGGED AT ME. I COULDN'T DO ANYTHING ABOUT IT UNTIL MORNING, AND THAT MADE IT EVEN WORSE.

THE KID AT SAFEWAY WOULDN'T JUST SELL ME AN EGG, SO I BOUGHT A DOZEN.

I PUT ONE IN MY POCKET, TOSSED THE REST, AND -- WHEN THE COAST WAS CLEAR-- WENT BACK TO THE APARTMENT.

IT FELT GOOD TO SOLVE A PROBLEM, TO MAKE SOMETHING RIGHT, NO MATTER HOW SMALL.

AFTER THAT, I GUESS I FELL INTO A ROUTINE JUST LIKE EVERYONE ELSE.

THE GUY AT THE BUBBLE TEA PLACE STARTED MAKING COFFEE AGAIN, JUST FOR ME.

SOME DAYS I'D BRING A LUNCH WITH ME, ALWAYS MAKING SURE TO CLEAN UP AND REMOVE ANY TRASH.

I SET THE ALARM ON
MY WATCH TO AVOID
ANY OVERLAP.

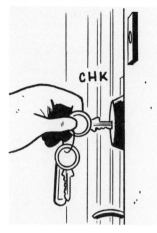

I SKETCHED A FLOOR-
PLAN AND WORKED
OUT SOME EXIT
STRATEGIES, JUST
IN CASE.

BUT FOR THE MOST
PART, IT'S HARD TO
SAY HOW I PASSED
THOSE HOURS, TO
BE HONEST.

THAT ONE DAY, I'D
ACTUALLY FALLEN
ASLEEP WHEN IT
ALL STARTED.

I ALMOST ANSWERED
THE DOOR OUT OF
HABIT.

IT WAS A KID, PROB-
ABLY HIGH SCHOOL
AGE. I FIGURED HE
WAS LOOKING FOR A
DONATION OR A
SIGNATURE ON A
PETITION.

HE RANG THE DOOR-
BELL A FEW TIMES,
THEN KNOCKED
AGAIN BEFORE
GIVING UP.

A FEW MINUTES
LATER, I HEARD THE
SCREEN FROM THE
BATHROOM WINDOW
CLATTERING INTO
THE BATHTUB.

BY THE TIME I GOT
THERE, THE KID WAS
HALFWAY THROUGH
THE WINDOW.

I REACTED ON PURE INSTINCT, LIKE IT WAS STILL MY HOME TO PROTECT.

IT FELT LIKE THE POWER COMING BACK ON AFTER A BLACKOUT.

I WAS A HUNDRED PERCENT IN THE RIGHT. WHATEVER HAPPENED, THE KID HAD IT COMING.

HE WAS SLOPPY AND SCARED, BUT HE MANAGED TO THINK ON HIS FEET.

IT WAS A GIFT--LIKE HE'D JUST GIVEN ME PERMISSION TO TURN IT UP A NOTCH.

STILL, I HELD BACK. THE LAST THING I NEEDED WAS AN AMBULANCE SHOWING UP THERE.

THE KID HAD ME OVER A BARREL AND HE DIDN'T EVEN KNOW IT.

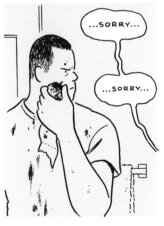

HE TRIED TO MAKE A BREAK FOR THE WINDOW, BUT BY THAT POINT HE WAS STRUGGLING.

I WALKED DOWN THE HALL AND OPENED THE BACK DOOR. COOL AIR BLEW IN FROM THE ALLEY.

GO AHEAD.

I DON'T KNOW WHAT I WAS EXPECTING, EXACTLY. DID HE UNDERSTAND HOW LUCKY HE WAS?

FUCK YOU, BITCH!

AFTER THAT IT WAS A RACE AGAINST THE CLOCK TO GET EVERY-THING BACK IN ORDER.

KLAK

IT TOOK LONGER THAN I EXPECTED, AND ALL I WANTED TO DO WAS GET OUT.

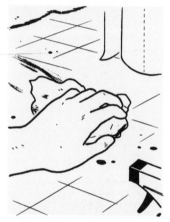

I WAS JUST ABOUT DONE WHEN I REAL-IZED I'D DEPLETED THE GUY'S CLEANING SUPPLIES.

IT WAS A LONG AFTERNOON.

BEEP BEEP BEEP

THE LAST DAY, I WAS LATER THAN USUAL.

I CAN'T REMEMBER HOW IT STARTED, BUT I GOT INTO A LITTLE SQUABBLE WITH THE GUY AT THE CAFE.

NO, NO, SIR... I AM BEING FRIENDLY!

HE MADE A COMMENT-- A LITTLE PASSIVE-AGGRESSIVE DIG-- AND AFTER ALL THE MONEY I'D PUT IN HIS COFFERS, IT BOTHERED ME.

MOST BUSINESSES VALUE A REGULAR CUSTOMER.

THE LIGHTS WERE ON IN THE APARTMENT WHEN I GOT THERE. THAT SHOULD'VE TIPPED ME OFF.

AS I MOVED TOWARD THE KITCHEN, I HEARD A SERIES OF SOUNDS: A THUD, SOMETHING CLATTERING ACROSS THE FLOOR, A MOAN.

SHE MUST'VE BEEN AT LEAST EIGHTY, MAYBE OLDER. WAS SHE THE GUY'S MOTHER? HIS GRANDMOTHER?

SHE STARTED SCREAMING IN SOME LANGUAGE I DIDN'T KNOW, AND SHE WOULDN'T STOP.

I TRIED TO HELP HER UP AND MAKE SURE SHE WASN'T HURT, BUT SHE KICKED AND SPAT AT ME AND SHRIEKED EVEN LOUDER.

I WANTED TO APOLOGIZE AND EXPLAIN EVERYTHING, BUT MOST OF ALL I WANTED TO DISAPPEAR.

I LOCKED THE DOOR BEHIND ME WHEN I LEFT. I LISTENED FOR SIRENS, ALMOST HOPING THAT I'D HEAR THEM.

I WALKED UP THE BLOCK, INTO THE STREAM OF OBLIVIOUS, HAPPY PEOPLE WITH THEIR FAMILIES, THEIR SHOPPING, THEIR CHATTER.

AND STARTING RIGHT THERE, I TRIED MY BEST TO BECOME ONE OF THEM.

121

ACKNOWLEDGMENTS

The quote on page 11 is from *The Isamu Noguchi Museum*, published by Harry N. Abrams, 1999. The lyrics on page 51 are a brief excerpt from the song "Starting a New Life," written by Van Morrison, copyright © 1971 Caledonia Soul Music Co., WB Music Corp. The jokes on pages 95 and 96 were originally performed by Ellen DeGeneres, Sarah Silverman, and Jerry Seinfeld.

The author would like to thank: Kathleen Alcott, Alexandra Auger, Jonathan Bennett, Peggy Burns, Daniel Clowes, Ann Cunningham, Tom Devlin, Mark Everett, Charles Ferraro, Denise Goldberg, Samantha J. Haywood, Mayumi Horiguchi, Tracy Hurren, Mina Kaneko, Daisuke Kawasaki, Keya Khayatian, Chip Kidd, John Kuramoto, Marie-Jade Menni, Françoise Mouly, Chris Oliveros, Mark Parker, Julia Pohl-Miranda, Jon Resnik, Richard Sala, Seth, Alyson Sinclair, Zadie Smith, Dylan Tomine, Chris Ware, John Wray, and most of all, Sarah, Nora, and May.

# Killing and Dying

 The material in this book was serialized in issues twelve through fourteen of *Optic Nerve* (published by Drawn & Quarterly). The story "Amber Sweet" originally appeared, under a different title and in substantially different form, in *Kramers Ergot* #7 (published by Buenaventura Press). 

www.drawnandquarterly.com
www.adrian-tomine.com

First hardcover edition: October 2015.
Printed in China.

10 9 8 7 6 5 4 3 2 1

Library and Archives Canada Cataloguing in Publication
Tomine, Adrian, 1974–, author, illustrator
*Killing and Dying* / Adrian Tomine.
ISBN 978-1-77046-209-0 (bound)
1. Graphic novels. I. Title.
PN6727.T65K55 2015 741.5'973 C2015-902360-2

Published in the USA by Drawn & Quarterly, a client publisher of Farrar, Straus and Giroux.
Orders: 888.330.8477

Published in Canada by Drawn & Quarterly, a client publisher of Raincoast Books.
Orders: 800.663.5714

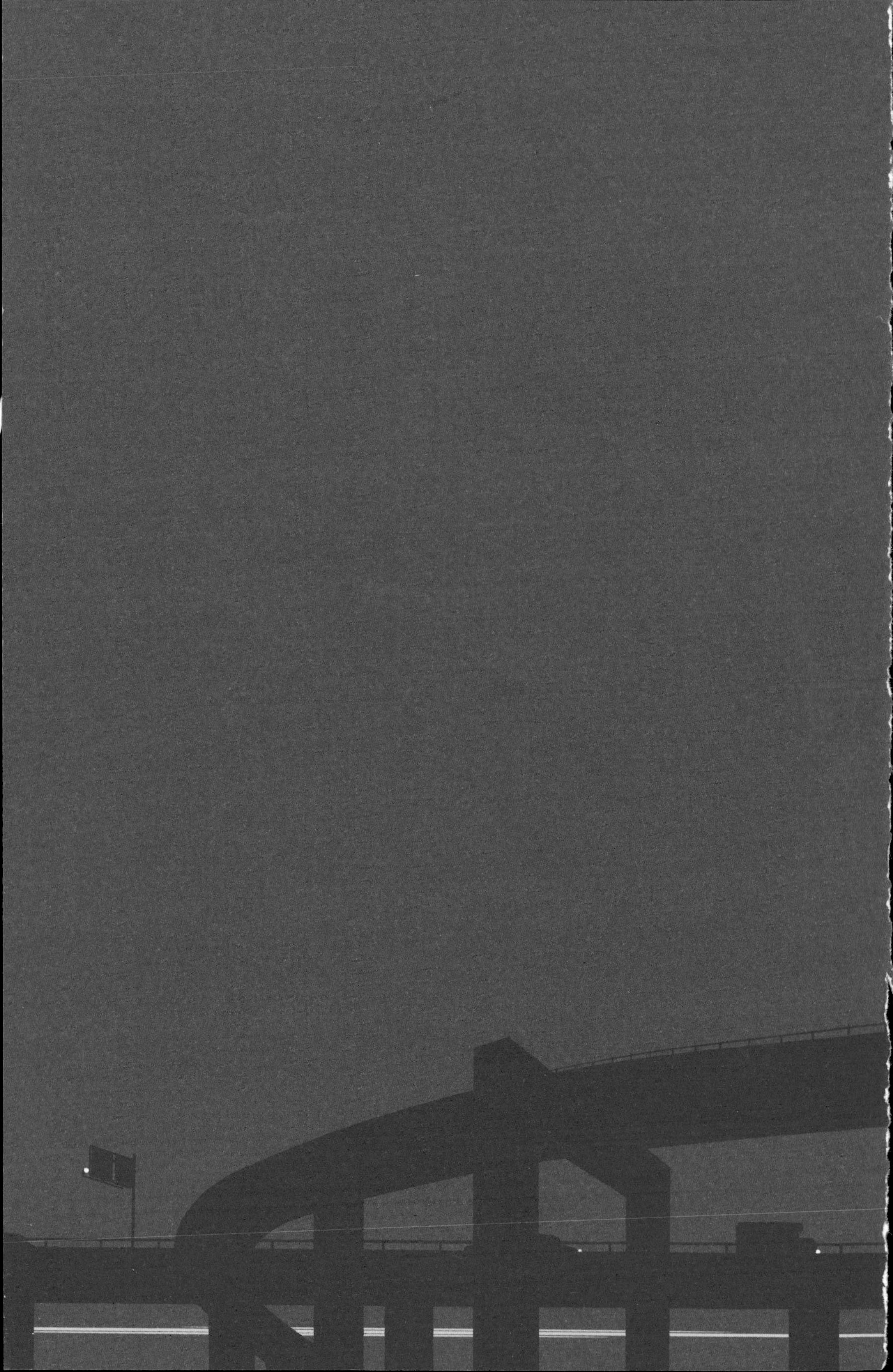